Australian Encounters

GHOSTS
DOWN UNDER

*

Barry Watts

'...the dreadful, hopeless howling of a lost soul...'

'she froze with fear when, close behind her,
footsteps crossed the veranda'

'the ghostly figure desperately kept his grip'

'neither whip nor spur would induce
their horses to cross the bridge'

'standing immediately behind him,
a misty green shadow outline of a human figure'

© Barry John Watts 2018

All rights reserved.

Without limiting the rights under copyright above, no part of this publication may be reproduced, stored in a retrieval system, or transmitted in any form or by any means [electronic, mechanical, photocopying, recording or otherwise] without the prior written permission of both the copyright holder and the publisher.

Published by Pegasus Education Group,
P.O. Box 223, McCrae, Victoria 3938, Australia

ISBN:978-0-9945355-9-7
First Printing: November 2018

Author contact:
barrywatts@bookfellows.com.au

CONTENTS

Introduction

1. **'UNFINISHED BUSINESS' AT THE ROCK** 1
   Hanging Rock, Victoria
2. **THE HAUNTED HILL** 11
   Bathurst Gold Escort, N.S.W.
3. **DON'T DISTURB THE DEAD** 15
   Pine Islet, Queensland
4. **A BLAST FROM THE PAST** 20
   Fort Nepean, Victoria
5. **SHOWERS OF WARM STONES** 23
   Mayanup, Western Australia
6. **SOLOMON WISEMAN'S WISDOM** 33
   Wiseman's Ferry, N.S.W.
7. **HE BEING DEAD, YET SPEAKETH** 37
   Port Arthur, Tasmania
8. **BRIDGE OVER HAUNTED WATERS** 46
   Wollongong, N.S.W.
9. **DEAD MAILMAN CALLS FOR 'HELP'** 49
   Burnett District, Queensland
10. **HOSTESS WITH THE GHOSTESS** 54
    Mt.Eliza & South Yarra, Victoria
11. **THE CONVICT'S REVENGE** 58
    Moreton Bay, Queensland
12. **A PITEOUS MOAN ... NO BULL!** 62
    Yass, N.S.W.
13. **OLD HENRY'S GHOST** 68
    Point Hicks, Victoria
14. **A CHINESE GIFT FOR LOVERS** 73
    Palmer River, Queensland
15. **THE MOST CELEBRATED GHOST** 79
    Campbelltown, N.S.W.
16. **SUFFER THE LITTLE CHILDREN** 86
    York, Western Australia

17. **A GHOSTLY NON-PAYING GUEST** **99**
    St.Kilda, Victoria
18. **A SPECTER IN LOINCLOTH AND TURBAN** **111**
    Launceston, Tasmania
19. **THE GUYRA POLTERGEIST** **114**
    Guyra, N.S.W.
20. **RESIDENT GHOST IN CELL 45** **123**
    Geelong, Victoria
21. **SHRIEKS IN THE NIGHT** **128**
    Prospect, South Australia
22. **PHANTOM OF A DIFFERENT OPERA** **132**
    Melbourne, Victoria
23. **GHOSTLY HOTSPOT** **141**
    Picton, N.S.W.
24. **DON'T MESS WITH 'HENRY'** **148**
    Yanchep, Western Australia
25. **BLUESTONE PUB SELLS SPIRITS** **155**
    Clarkefield, Victoria
26. **THE GHOST WHO ROCKS** **161**
    Port Arthur, Tasmania
27. **COUNTING MONTE CRISTO'S GHOSTS** **165**
    Junee, N.S.W.
28. **A GHOST ON THE BRIDGE** **173**
    Pinjarrah, Western Australia
29. **'I'M RELATED TO YOUR GHOST'** **178**
    Toowoomba, Queensland
30. **VIOLENCE FROM BEYOND** **184**
    Ararat, Victoria
31. **A HITCH-HIKING GHOST** **190**
    Jenolan Caves, N.S.W.
32. **A GHOST MAY BE HEARD** **199**
    Central West, Queensland

References Consulted **208**

ACKNOWLEDGEMENTS

The author gratefully acknowledges the assistance provided by numerous people and organizations during the compilation of this book, without which some of the ghostly encounters included here would not be accessible.

In particular, my gratitude goes to my colleague, Sandy Coghlan, for her 'Introduction' to this book; the staff of the Mornington Peninsula Library Service (particularly 'L.G.' of Information Services); and multiple librarians at various State and Regional Libraries around Australia (*'Ask a Librarian'*).

The services of the National Library of Australia (with emphasis on their *Trove* facility) have greatly assisted with the gathering of published data – from both books and newspapers.

Utilized sources are identified in the text either immediately before or after their inclusion in this work. A full list of 'References Consulted' also appears at the back of this publication.

IMPORTANT MESSAGE

Several places mentioned in this book are privately owned and do not welcome ghost-seeking visitors, photographers or stickybeaks. We suggest you check websites to establish accessibility, opening hours, entry fees / tour times before leaving home.

INTRODUCTION

According to the Encyclopedia Britannica, a ghost is a ... soul or specter of a dead person, usually believed to inhabit the netherworld and capable of returning in some form to the world of the living.

Netherworld? Most dictionaries define the netherworld as hell or Hades, and it's certainly true that some ghosts appear angry and revengeful. Such lost souls, however, may not be 'returning to the world of the living' but are literally trapped here. They may be fearful of moving on, certain they're destined for hell, thereby creating their own version of hell through voluntary imprisonment.

One such soul you will meet in this book spent most of his life in a Victorian prison. Foul-mouthed and quick-tempered, he refused to move on after death, choosing to remain in the same cell in the same prison, fiercely protecting his territory and aggressively intimidating any who dare to invade it.

Others fear retribution because they committed the sin of taking their own life. One nineteenth century military officer haunts a bridge that horses later refused to cross at night. The officer had been supervising convicts in its construction, but chose to leave this world by his own hand after shaming himself while drunk.

Perhaps the most poignant case Barry Watts presents in his intriguing book deals with the plight of numerous lost souls awaiting release at a famous location in Victoria. The site became known world-wide when a multi-award winning movie was set there in the 1970's. Many later questioned whether the story—based on a popular book—was fact or fiction. Although both book and subsequent movie were presented as fiction, the opening chapter of Ghosts Down Under reveals there may be more truth to it than most readers and movie-goers guessed.

While lost souls and angry ghosts are frightening to those who encounter them, they usually do no harm. But then there are poltergeists!

The word poltergeist is derived from two German words—poltern (crash) and geist (ghost). In other words, a poltergeist is a noisy and mischievous or angry ghost (depending on the level of activity) that can throw things around, create noise, levitate objects—and sometimes even people—and basically cause havoc. It tends to focus on one person, usually a female adolescent, and is often dismissed as merely 'hormonal activity'.

How hormones can perform such functions is anyone's guess, but a deceased Scottish woman named Dorcas, communicating through the mediumship of Englishman Leslie Flint in 1964, may provide us with a clue about poltergeists. After passing in the 1700's, Dorcas initially felt more comfortable remaining on earth than moving on. She was eventually encouraged to leave the lower realms, but while earthbound, she amused herself by scaring people:

'I used to play pranks. I used to do all sorts of things. I used to get quite a great deal of fun and pleasure out of that; opening and shutting doors, and throwing coal and all sorts of things, breaking mirrors, and frightening people.'

When asked how it was possible to move physical objects without a physical body, Dorcas replied:

'There's lots of different ways when you know how to do it. Providing the power is there, but you've got to find someone who's got the power and vitality, usually when there's children present it's easier. It's no good using old people, as a rule. They've got no vitality or power. You can't draw from them at all.'

Dorcas, it seems, was a poltergeist merely because she was bored!

The first poltergeist on record is said to have occurred in Germany in 856AD. It tormented the family living there by throwing stones and starting fires. Two more stone-throwing poltergeists are included in this book. These occurred thirty years apart and on opposites sides of the continent, and both made newspaper headlines at the time.

One, in 1921, took place in New South Wales at the home of a 12-year old girl. Stones were constantly thrown on and inside the house, and were often accompanied by loud rapping on the walls.

Another incident took place at the home of an indigenous family in Western Australia in the 1950's. This time, the stones were warm! Again, they were not confined to the roof and exterior walls, but also flew across rooms inside the house. One even landed in a glass of beer!

Not all ghosts, though, are mischievous or angry. Some may not even be ghosts at all, but merely emotional imprint manifestations. These can occur when a traumatic experience has taken place, and the emotion felt at the time was so intense that an echo of the experience remains to replay itself over and over again. In these cases, the apparition does not respond to the living.

We have all heard stories of headless ghosts on horseback galloping across castle courtyards at midnight on full moon nights. While this book does not include tales of this nature, such echoes do often imprint themselves in brutal prisons and poorly-run mental hospitals. Keep an eye open for some of those in the following pages.

The sweetest ghosts are those who are simply drawn to earth because they have a fondness for a certain place or person. These are probably the most common sightings, but sadly, they are rarely discussed by the person being visited for fear of ridicule and disbelief.

According to the British Medical Journal, a recent survey of widows and widowers in the UK revealed that almost half those interviewed confessed to having seen their deceased husband or wife within ten years of their spouses' death. In almost every case, these were benevolent visits which brought much comfort to those left behind.

While Barry's book does not deal with individual visitations, he has included instances of those who return or remain simply because they enjoy being here.

One is particularly famous amongst theatre-goers. He's a 19th century stage actor who has often been observed, dressed in his finery, applauding from beyond the stage at a well-known Melbourne theatre. For many years, a seat was even left vacant for this phantom thespian on opening night!

You will also find the story of Australia's most famous ghost, who returned to play a part in helping the police solve his own murder. Then there's the ghost at a popular tourist attraction who returned to clear his good name, another who saved the lives of a pair of love-struck runaways.

Some are stories are best read at night around a campfire, or by torchlight under a blanket. Others will warm your heart and may provide a whole new perspective on ghosts.

Australia's most famous song, Waltzing Matilda, includes the line: ...and his ghost may be heard as you pass by the billabong'. This wonderful book by Barry Watts may provide comfort for many Aussie ghosts by allowing them to tell their stories ... so they may be heard.

Sandy Coghlan

(Author: *Heaven Knows*)

1. 'Unfinished Business' at the Rock

'...the dreadful, hopeless howling of a lost soul...'

Geologists will tell you that Hanging Rock in regional Victoria is neither a small mountain nor a large hill.

It's ... well, ah ...unusual.

'The Rock' stands just 100m (a little over 300ft) above the adjoining farming land. Six million years ago it was thrust up through the Earth's surface as a mixture of lava and rock, solidifying as it cooled and weathered into large vertical slabs and columns.

Hanging Rock

Over eons it has been exposed to weathering and erosion,

resulting in a conglomeration of unusual rock formations. It has tall trees growing among soil and scattered rocks for half its height (as far as the 'Platform'), but its uppermost half is almost naked of vegetation, leaving the bare tops of huge, fissured, rocks pointing skyward.

Many visitors admit to being 'spooked' as they climb towards its summit. They report an eerie feeling of being 'watched' or supervised by an invisible 'somebody' or 'something'. Some get chills on warm sunny days, others hear voices when there's no one else around.

Best-selling paranormal writer, the late Dawn Hill, recalled a visit she made to Hanging Rock in the 1980s:

> In places, as you walk, it is possible to hear a sepulchral echo of your footsteps underneath the stone surface. The place has an atmosphere of brooding mystery ... [Dawn Hill, Edge of Reality, Pan Books, 1987, p.253]

Hanging Rock has strong links with pre-European indigenous people. Its original custodians, the Wurundjeri, shared its lower slopes with neighboring clan-groups for social and trading purposes. Their practices at the weathered volcanic outcrop ensured stability across territorial borders.

> Standing at the juncture of lands familiar to three distinct peoples of Aboriginal Australia, it was always a place for their ceremonial events, a meeting place of different networks, and the site for bartering for greenstone* the crossroads for trade routes that extended across what are now state borders... [Chris McConville, Hanging Rock – a History, Melbourne, 2017, p. 16]. * a hand-held stone used like an axe head

Spiritualists have also long been interested in the unusual effects permeating the Rock. Almost a century-and-a-half ago (1874) the *Mount Alexander Mail* announced:

SPIRITUALIST PICNIC

> It has been arranged that the Spiritualist's Picnic at the Hanging Rock, Woodend shall take place on Sunday, December 6th. Special trains have been granted by the department. It is said that from Sandhurst [Bendigo] alone there will be 2,000 visitors, while from Castlemaine it is estimated the number will be about 300.

Also in the late nineteenth century, local families began a pattern which has continued, in magnified form, to this day:

> ... farming families had begun to gather on flat land beneath Hanging Rock, for Christmas and New Year get-togethers ... [By 1884] Hanging Rock had become a spectacular summer fairground. Much of this was due to the popularity of the Hanging Rock horse races, held each New Year's Day. [Chris McConville, Hanging Rock – A History, (Melbourne, 2017), p. 9]

Horse racing continues into the 21st century, and global entertainers such as Leonard Cohen, Rod Stewart, Bruce Springsteen and Ed Sherran have presented open-air concerts at Hanging Rock's 'East Paddock'.

Indigenous ceremonies, rock concerts, spiritualist picnics, horse-races? Strange bedfellows indeed.

What is it that draws them all to this semi-naked hill of lava and rock jutting skywards just 77kms (48miles) from cosmopolitan Melbourne?

It was a book, Picnic at Hanging Rock, that ultimately altered the reputation of the landmark.

> Unless you have been living under, well, a rock, you would have heard at least a smidgen of the story that has haunted the country's collective psyche for more than half a century: a small party of girls and teachers from hoity-toity Appleyard College set out in the searing heat for a Valentine's Day picnic at Hanging Rock in 1900. Some never returned. [Anna Byrne, 'Rock On', Herald Sun Weekend Magazine, 28 April 2018, p. 04]

The book was written by Joan Lindsay and first

published in 1967 when she was in her early 70s. She was related to the Boyd family of artists and writers, and became a member of the creative Lindsay family when she married Daryl Lindsay (later knighted) in London on 14 February 1922 – Valentine's Day.

Why did Joan Lindsay choose this site as the setting for her book? And why did her book and the subsequent movie so firmly etch themselves into the global psyche?

'Joan was known to be a mystic,' her biographer Janelle McCulloch is quoted as saying, 'Her friends firmly believed she had this extraordinary affinity with the landscape, and could 'read' it like Indigenous Australians do; and see things in it that we can't.'

Here is an oft-quoted example of Joan Lindsay's clairvoyance, as published in her biography:

> On one occasion, in 1929, she was driving to Creswick [her husband's birthplace] with Daryl to visit his family when she noticed several nuns running through a field. They seemed to be running from something. One of the nuns appeared to be wearing burned clothing, and when Joan looked back, at the landscape behind them, she could see what appeared to be a burning building.
>
> When she mentioned it to Daryl, he was amazed. He hadn't seen a thing. She immediately knew that the scene did not belong in the present time.
>
> When they arrived at Creswick she discovered that a convent had existed on that side of town, but that it had burned down several years earlier. It was then she realized she had somehow been transported back to that time, albeit for a brief moment. [Janelle McCulloch, Beyond the Rock: The Life of Joan Lindsay and the Mystery of Picnic at Hanging Rock, Echo Publishing, 2017, pps. 141-142]

Did Joan's clairvoyance reveal things about Hanging Rock to her that inspired her to write the book? Did she know what happened to the missing girls and teacher after their picnic at Hanging Rock?

Some of the readers of Joan Lindsay's book felt short-changed. There were too many unanswered questions... were the girls abducted, or worse, murdered? If so, by whom? Were they ever found? Readers wanted to know, as well, if the book was based on historical fact?

Sandra Forbes—the book's original editor at F W Cheshire Joan Lindsay's Melbourne publisher—was asked much later, if she thought it was true.

> 'Joan was Lady Lindsay by this point, and a prominent figure in Melbourne society,' remembers Sandra. 'She was very intelligent, and very elegant. She took me to lunch one day, at her club, the Lyceum Club in Melbourne ...
>
> Did I think the story was true? We did talk about this. But the truth for Joan was different to the rest of us. She was never straightforward about it. I think I decided in the end that it was a great work of the imagination. [Janelle McCulloch, Beyond the Rock, p.151]

In the early 1970s, Sydney-based film producer and actress Pat Lovell acquired the film rights to *Picnic at Hanging Rock*. Peter Weir was her nominated director, with screenplay by David Williamson.

Williamson soon found he was over committed by other projects and suggested Cliff Green as screenwriter.

Joan Lindsay's agreement to sell the film rights ensured that she retained her right to approve both director and screenwriter. Meetings with Peter Weir and Cliff Green were arranged. She met Cliff Green in the ABC's Melbourne studios at Ripponlea, where a string of fortuitous coincidents were quickly revealed.

Cliff Green lived at Warrandyte on the Yarra River, on Melbourne's northern outskirts. Joan had lived at Warrandyte after she left art school. 'You must live near my cousin Penliegh Boyd,' she said. Cliff did. Then she mentioned the Woodend storekeeper, Mr Hussey, who is in her book. Mr Hussey was Cliff Green's son-in-law's grandfather!

Cliff then told Joan he had adapted a Norman Lindsay (her brother-in-law) book to the screen, and her cousin Martin Boyd's novel *Lucinda Brayford* for the BBC. 'Joan thought that all these connections and coincidences were completely natural, part of life's magnificent tapestry,' Cliff Green said. She gave him the nod of approval.

Cliff had been warned earlier not to ask Joan if the *'Picnic'* story was true. He asked anyway:

> Her stock answer was: 'Some of it is true and some of it isn't.' In the end I decided that fiction and facts had been woven so inextricably together that it was impossible, even for her, to distinguish the difference. [Cliff Green, in Janelle McCulloch, Beyond the Rock, p.156]

Peter Weir, the director, promptly met Joan's approval, too—coincidentally, his middle name is 'Lindsay'.

Much of the film *'Picnic at Hanging Rock'* was shot on-site at Hanging Rock. Two interesting anecdotes – each with a spooky 'wow' effect – happened during filming at the Rock.

Firstly, co-producer Pat Lovell remembered:

> The Rock started having an effect on all our lives. My watch stopped entirely and our alarm clocks seemed to go off at different times, while quite often on the Rock there was an overpowering feeling of being suspended in time. So Joan Lindsay's magic references to the Rock are probably true. [Patricia Lovell, No Picnic, An Autobiography, (Macmillan, 1995), p.159]

Next, Anne-Louise Lambert who played one of the missing girls, Miranda, in the movie tells how, during a break on the set, she had wandered off into the bush in costume when she saw Joan Lindsay slowly coming towards her:

> I went to hold out my hand but she walked straight up to me, put her arms around me, and said in a very emotional way: 'Oh Miranda, it's been so long!'

> She was shaking like a leaf. I wasn't sure what to do, so I said very politely 'It's me Joan, it's Anne. It's so nice to meet you.' But she dismissed this with a wave of her hand.

> She just said 'Miranda' again, and clung on me, and so I embraced her back. I think we both started to cry. It was very moving. And it was clear she'd regressed into some part of her past. To her, I really was someone she had known, somewhere in time…There was certainly something very true about the scenes we were

filming on the Rock, and the story itself, not just the facts but also the meaning for Joan. [Anne-Louise Lambert, in Janelle McCulloch, Beyond the Rock, p.161]

As Lindsay's editor, Sandra Forbes' commented: '...the truth for Joan was different to the rest of us.'

When released in August 1975, the film *Picnic at Hanging Rock* was acclaimed both locally and overseas, as an outstanding achievement, winning 'Best Cinematography' awards in the U.K. and the USA, and 'Best Film' from the Australia Film Institute.

It is intriguing to reflect that viewers world-wide referred to the movie and its pan flute musical score as 'haunting'.

Over a decade after 'Picnic' was released, Dawn Hill (mentioned at the beginning of this chapter) and her husband, Roland, a deep trance medium, visited the rock to film a paranormal video documentary.

When they arrived, their crew was waiting for them. It was a sullen, late-winter morning as Dawn and Roland set off to climb the pinnacles and seek out an area that 'felt right' for filming. They climbed the path through the trees for twenty minutes and had almost reached half-way when Roland took off on a sidetrack to the left and disappeared from view behind a cluster of large boulders.

Dawn called for Roland to come back to the main track. He didn't respond. Next, she glimpsed him through a narrow fissure in a huge boulder, he was moving in a deep trance, like a sleepwalker. She quickly joined him. Roland was drawn to a huge monolith which, three meters above the surface, had a large cavity that he felt compelled to enter.

'Help me, Dawn! I've got to get in there,' he cried.

'...I gave him a leg up, and then braced myself while he took my shoulder for a foothold to reach the small cave.

I stepped back to watch as Roland crawled into a sitting position within the hollowed-out stone, sobbing, and muttering to himself all the while. Then involuntarily, I held my breath. The face that looked out blindly from within the stone was not the face of my husband.

> As the first tormented howls shattered the frozen silence, I knew what I was hearing. There is no other sound that strikes the vitals with quite the same impact as the dreadful, hopeless howling of a lost soul...' [Dawn Hill, Edge of Reality, Pan Books, 1987, pps. 260-1]

Dawn immediately called on her own spirit guide, David, for help, concentrating her mind on a single command: 'Peace be still.'

Moments later the anguished cries from the cave abated as Roland's face softened, and Dawn recognized the characteristic body rhythms that signaled David's arrival. The words 'My daughter, I am David,' greeted Dawn, 'That one is with me.'

> If the rescue had been completed and all the lost souls gathered up, or if there has only been one in the vicinity, David will say 'It is done,' signifying that the atmosphere around us is now clear.
>
> 'Are there more?' I asked. He nodded, 'There are many'...
>
> 'What is this place?'
>
> 'It is a congregation area,' came the answer from David ...
>
> 'How many could we help?'
>
> 'As many as this man could take,' he replied, indicating Roland's body with a brief gesture.
>
> I could only answer with a philosophical shrug, 'Okay, you know the limits. Whenever you're ready.'
>
> 'Now is not the time, my daughter. This man will sleep.' Roland's head dropped forward onto his chest and I turned to face the wide-eyed film crew.
>
> 'What you have just seen is a psychic rescue.' I explained the procedure to them briefly before turning to offer my shoulder to Roland, now awake and indicating that he wished to climb down.
> [Dawn Hill, Edge of Reality, Pan Books, 1987, pps. 261-2]

Portions of this psychic rescue at Hanging Rock are included in the Andronicus Foundation video 'Who Speaks?', which features Roland and Dawn Hill, and others. It was published in the late 1980s and is now becoming difficult to obtain.

Unaware of Dawn and Roland Hill's experiences, another

later group of visitors also sensed – or perhaps even saw – lost souls gathered at Hanging Rock. Park Ranger Guido Bigolin recalls:

> A group of tough, courageous Indigenous Australians from the Northern Territory began to venture up the rock. This group didn't even get halfway. They were clearly edgy on the ascent, and as they approached the halfway mark they turned in their tracks and ran down the hill…
>
> They ran back to the car park and jumped back in the bus as fast as they could …
>
> All they would say was, 'This is an evil place! There is unfinished business here!' [Park Ranger Guido Bigolin in Janelle McCulloch's Beyond the Rock, Echo Publishing, 2017, p.xvii]

It would seem that Hanging Rock is a point where earth-bound spirits and lost souls gather to await release or 'rescue'. Perhaps many people – such as the Indigenous Australians and Joan Lindsay – have intuitively known this all along.

In 2018 the Hanging Rock legend was re-ignited:

> Now, a new Foxtel mini-series will sustain the legend for a new generation, triggering the country's, and arguably, the world's, fascination with the rock once again. And there is no denying that the story's misperceived foothold in reality has only added to its potency over the years…
>
> The new mini-series, with six hours to tell the story as opposed to Weir's running time of one hour and 55 minutes, will further delve into the vortex of women in the Hanging Rock story. [Anne Byrne, 'Rock On', Herald Sun Weekend magazine, 28 April 2018, pps 4-5]

Helping to sustain the newsworthiness of the 2018 mini-series release, the *Sunday Herald Sun* (Melbourne) posed this question:

CAN PSYCHICS UNLOCK HANGING ROCK'S ENDURING, MYSTERIOUS PRESENCE?

> This week we invited a group of spiritual authorities including celebrity psychic Harry T, Amazonian tribal medicine woman Antonia Ruhl, Native American healer Red Horse, and members of Aussie Down Under Paranormal Investigations to visit the Rock and share their findings.

Some detected an abduction of a group of innocent girls in the late 1800s, others spoke of the rocks as a place of joy that was filled with the spirit of happy children. All agreed it was a powerful, spiritual and sacred place just as it is for the three indigenous nations who are custodians of the land ... [Catherine Lambert, 'Secrets in the Stone,' Sunday Herald Sun, 29 April 2018, p.23]

Members of the three indigenous nations sharing custody of the Rock were also invited to participate. They declined.

Gary Pendlebury of Aussie Down Under Paranormal Investigations used a K2 meter to detect changes in the electromagnetic fields on Hanging Rock:

'It was off scale,' Pendlebury said. 'We say that is a Class A validation of spirits being present, and the level was unprecedented.' ...he and his team also sensed many cold spots while climbing the rock, which he said indicated ghost activity. [Gary Pendlebury, Sunday Herald Sun, 29 April 2018, p.23]

Antonia Ruhl, tribal medicine woman, sensed the presence of spirits of both children and adults:

'... there were a lot of happy kids the higher I climbed. I was asked by a lot of little kids to go into a cave – asking me to come and play. I sat there and was going further in when an adult lady said, 'Don't go there.'

Antonia didn't proceed further: 'I had various spirits communicating with me,' celebrity psychic Harry T said, 'I felt the presence of so many children who are so linked to the place.'

Harry T also sensed the presence of a woman:

'I picked up on a woman spirit who acknowledged herself as a psychic, and I wonder if she was the author of the book – now that I know about it.' [Harry T, *Sunday Herald Sun*, 29 April 2018, p.23]

Site details: https://www.mountmacedon.org.au/places/hanging-rock-reserve

2. The Haunted Hill

This is a hill that has long been known to spook horses and make grown men shiver.

Wyagdon Hill …has been known as 'The Haunted Hill' for three-quarters of a century.

The strange caperings of horses from time to time when crossing it keeps the superstition alive, and there are many local people who prefer a roundabout route to riding over it at night. [Sydney Mail, 31 July 1935, p.42]

It has long been accepted that animals possess the faculty of second-sight.

Drovers believe that horses and cattle see things that humans cannot, and those who know the roads avoid camps that have a reputation of being haunted. There are many such places on the main stock routes in the back country…[Sydney Mail, 31 July 1935, p.42]

In an article for English magazine Pearson's early last century, English author and policeman Elliott O'Donnell recalled…

I have on several occasions been riding through very lonely districts in the dead of night when my horse has suddenly halted, shied, shivered, and manifested symptoms of the utmost terror. I have seen nothing myself, but I have invariably discovered afterwards that the spots where the horse underwent these experiences were reputed to be haunted, or were close to the site of a 'barrow' or some kind of burial place, or were immediately associated with some grim tragedy. [Extracted from Newcastle Morning Herald, 11 August 1917, p. 13]

O'Donnell's observations certainly hold true at Wyagdon Hill. Situated on the road north from Bathurst to Sofala and the old Turon goldfields in New South Wales, it is a hill that has long been known to 'spook' horses and make grown men shiver.

What happened on Wyagdon Hill that cause humans to avoid it and horses to bolt?

Wyagdon in particular was a haven for robbers preying on individual travelers as they breathlessly struggled to the top – for at that time the road ran straight up the hill, unlike the present road which winds up its side. [Matthew Higgins, Canberra Times, 25 February 1984, p. 15]

During the gold rush in the 1850's, over 7,000 people flocked to the area to make their fortune, but transporting their riches from such a remote area to the safety of banks at Bathurst, 28 miles (45 kms) away was a fearful venture.

Mounted police—known as the 'Gold Police'—were employed to escort the gold-laden coach between rural towns and their nearest larger towns or cities. At least one of these armed guards sat beside the coach-driver, another rode ahead, more stayed close to the coach.

On December 22nd, 1857, the rostered advanced guard for the 'Gold Coach' was Robert Codrington, a 23-year-old Englishman. On that fateful morning, he harnessed up his horse and kissed his wife goodbye, little knowing it was for the last time.

It was his duty to meet the gold escort with its accompanying patrol of troopers as they came up out of the Turon valley, to act as an advance guard by riding some distance ahead of the coach as it made the formidable Wyagdon descent. [Matthew Higgins, Canberra Times, 25 February 1984, p.15]

Bathurst Gold Escort, N.S.W.

Codrington arrived at the usual meeting place on Wyagdon Hill, unaware that the gold coach had been delayed for more than half an hour. He remained mounted and listened intently for its approach.

As he waited, something unusual caught his eye and alerted him to possible danger. A barricade of freshly-cut tree branches had been constructed on the edge of the track.

He quietly dismounted, slipped his carbine from his saddle holster with one hand and drew his pistol with the other.

Slowly, silently, he stepped towards the piled foliage.

Robert Codrington was hit with a hail of buckshot and bullets at close range. He fell lifeless to the ground. His horse, unscathed during the incident, reared and turned, bolting back the way it had come.

The robbers scattered and ran when armed guards on the approaching Gold Coach, alerted by the noise, opened fire.

> The ill fated man, who has been missing since Tuesday morning, his horse having returned to the Police Station without him, was discovered after a lengthy search by Sergeant Giles, lying head foremost down the hill, with his arms outstretched, and his feet carefully placed together. [Bathurst Free Press, 26 December 1857, p. 2]

Today, horses still become fractious when passing this area near the top of Wyagdon Hill.

Do they see the ambush taking place over and over again?

Does a ghostly horse bolt in panic through the trees towards them?

Or perhaps it's not only the echoes of Codrington's bloodthirsty murder that spooks the horses today. Every trip made by the Gold Coach was a fearful necessity. To those who lurked in the shadows, the guard's lives were far less valuable than a bag of gold dust. Danger lay hidden at every turn, behind every tree, over every rise.

GHOSTS DOWN UNDER

As they crossed Wyagdon Hill, the nervous guards would have needed to stay alert throughout the journey. They would be watching for any slight movement, peering intently at every possible hiding place, listening carefully for any unusual sound.

Echoes of such intense emotion may still permeate Wyagdon Hill to this day, creating a cheerless shroud of anxiety felt by man and beast.

☼

3. Don't Disturb the Dead

'she froze with fear when, close behind her, footsteps crossed the verandah

Pine Islet is on the mainland side of Middle Island. It is a single, steep granite rock rising to about 70 meters (230ft) height, with a deep crevice cutting into it. Hoop pines grow out of the rock on one side, the lighthouse and its cottages (built in 1885) straddle the other side. A steep ladder stairway was built on both faces of the crevice to assist the inhabitants move across the small 50-acre island.

> The inhabitants of Pine Islet are quite a small colony, three men, two having wives & children, thirteen persons in all. Their quarters are spacious and comfortable, perched high above the sea on the brink of a precipice. Through the windows you got charming glimpses of the sea and islands. [N. Rogers, 'A New Year Cruise on the Queensland Coast , c. 1888, page 9]

William McKay was the first Head Light-keeper. He and his wife Dorothea lived in the Head Keeper's cottage until tragedy struck in January 1895. Dorothea died of cancer. She was buried on a small piece of the remaining flat land quite close to the island's second cottage. William placed a marble slab over her sunken coffin and built a picket fence around all four sides of the grave.

Dorothea McKay rested peacefully in her carefully tended grave for over three decades.

In 1927, however, Dorothea's final resting place was disturbed. The old cottages surrounding her grave site were replaced with three fibro-clad buildings. This required the relocation of her grave to an area thirty meters (98ft) away. During this process, it was discovered that the much of the coffin had disintegrated, and the marble slab had cracked from one end to the other.

Although the workmen respectfully re-interred the remains in the new grave and covered it with a new and suitably inscribed marble slab, its replacement may have been the final indignity for Dorothea.

The Braid family lived on Pine Islet in the 1970's. Gordon Braid was lighthouse keeper, and lived in the cottage with his family. Their children recall many encounters with the ghost of Dorothea.

Apparently, Dorothea disliked the new arrangements. Or maybe it was the new marble slab she objected to, as Peter Braid recalls hearing that her ghost made its first appearance shortly after the original slab was replaced.

Pine Islet, Queensland

When the lighthouse keeper moved into the new cottage built over the old grave, strange things began to happen. Invisible knuckles rapped loudly on the front door, then footsteps and faint muttering sounds (indecipherable but clearly angry) were heard inside the cottage. [Richard Davis, Great Australian Ghost Stories, (Sydney, 2012). p.268]

Over the following fifty years or more, the various Pine Islet lighthouse keepers and their staff eventually grew familiar with the restless antics of Dorothea McKay. Knocks on the door were mostly ignored, footsteps and angry mutterings were accepted as perfectly normal.

Peter Braid's sister, Sharon, writes of some of other strange occurrences during their time in the lighthouse keeper's cottage...

We lived in the haunted house on Pine Islet ... every night my mother would close the doors of the cupboards throughout the house and in the morning they would all be open again. I'm not sure who started it, but they were known as coffin cupboards!
[Sharon Fielden, Haunted: The Book of Australia's Ghosts by John Pinkney]

Peter Braid adds ...

There was one room in particular in the house that she seemed to prefer and we were led to believe that it was over the top of her original grave site. [Peter Braid, Haunted: The Book of Australia's Ghosts by John Pinkney]

During their final four-months stint on Pine Islet as relief light-keepers Stuart & Shirley Buchanan also heard stories about Dorothea's ghostly appearances:

Time and time again, footsteps were heard on the concrete path outside the cottage, but when investigated no-one could be seen ...families of lightkeepers, many of them with no prior knowledge of Dorothea's disinterment, or the well-known belief that if a body is moved from its proper resting place the spirit becomes restless and returns to the place it knew in life, have reported these strange occurrences to the Head Lightkeeper of the time.

A few years ago, while a Lightkeeper was on his nightly watch at the tower, his wife, determined to discover who or what was causing the knocking, sat in a chair on the verandah beside the closed front door and waited nervously for something to happen.

Eventually she heard three distinct knocks.

With pounding heart she wrenched herself from the chair, flung open the door and saw – absolutely nothing; but she froze with fear when, close behind her, footsteps crossed the verandah, and slowly faded away into the house. [Stuart Buchanan, The Lighthouse Keepers, Samford. Qld., 1997, p.251]

When their term as relief lighthouse keepers was over and Head Lightkeeper Dudley returned, Shirley Buchanan asked him if he believed these stories.

He replied hesitantly:

Well – I didn't, but about a year ago a relief light-keeper who I knew very well moved into No.2 cottage. He told me that one evening when he was sitting watching television he heard footsteps on the verandah.

'Hello, is that you, Dudley?' he called. But no-one answered.

He was just about to stand up and go out to the verandah when the footsteps entered the lounge room, passed between him and the television set and continued on into the kitchen where they suddenly stopped.

Now if anyone else had told me that, I wouldn't have believed them – but this chap wasn't the type to make up such a story. [Buchanan, The Lighthouse Keepers, p.251]

The Buchanan's stay on Pine in cottage No. 2 passed without any known visits from Dorothea's ghost. Shirley appeared quite disappointed about this, and her husband Stuart teased her by suggesting 'Perhaps she went on holidays with the lightkeepers' [who they were relieving]. Shirley was unimpressed by his comment.

However, Shirley had the last say ...

A few weeks later [Stuart wrote], I sent three rolls of film away for processing. Of the hundred or so color transparencies we received back, all were perfect except four – they were blurred and double exposed. I put it down to just a coincidence that the four shots were the only ones I had taken of No. 2 cottage and Dorothea's headstone.

'On holidays, was she?' Shirley remarked smugly. [Buchanan, The Lighthouse Keepers, p.252]

Pine Islet, Queensland

The Pine Islet Lighthouse was decommissioned on 27 August 1985 – a hundred years after it was built. It was replaced by a 6m high fiberglass tower without a lamp and serves as an automated daymark (daytime identifier)

Darrell Roche was the last lighthouse keeper on Pine Islet. He relocated in 1985. As he packed his belongings and no doubt reminded himself to 'turn off all the lights on the way out', he fondly recalled his last encounter with Dorothea McKay ...

> 'The last time she came was about eighteen months ago. There was no knock on the door, only footsteps through the cottage into the lounge room. There she stopped – above her original grave – and we've never heard anything from her since.' [Richard Davis, Great Australian Ghost Stories, Sydney, 2012. p.268]

It's intriguing to note that by this time, Dorothea no longer felt the need to knock before entering. Perhaps she was relieved the new-comers were preparing to leave at last and her home could be her own again.

Her original grave site is now unencumbered by a cottage, and one can only hope that after almost six decades, Dorothea McKay has at last found the peace she sought on the isolated, wind-swept rock called Pine Islet.

☼

4. A Blast from the Past

'Then I saw a black shadow person with red eyes, sticking its head around a corner, looking at us!'

To reach Melbourne by sea, ships enter Port Phillip Bay from Bass Strait through 'The Rip' – a narrow, treacherous stretch of water. The drowned hulk of many a vessel lies rotting on the sea bed near this shallow entrance.

Reefs projecting from Point Nepean on the east and Point Lonsdale on the western side reduce the practical navigable width of 'The Rip' to less than 1.5 kilometers.

Even the mighty navigator Matthew Flinders ran aground here back in 1802. Fortunately, he was able to free his ship—*The Investigator*—and complete the first detailed examination of the Bay and its surrounding countryside.

Since then, at least 50 other vessels have been less fortunate and are now magnets for adventurous scuba divers.

Is The Rip itself haunted? And if so, is it the ghost of a drowned sailor, a captain who chose to go down with his floundering ship, or a hapless passenger flung overboard as the ship ran aground?

All we know is that at least one red-eyed 'shadow person' guards the tunnels in the limestone cliffs at Point Nepean—an area purposefully set up to guard The Rip and prevent unwanted guests.

Fort Nepean, Victoria

Our colonial forefathers recognized that the narrow entrance provided an ideal site for a series of military installations to protect Melbourne from sea-borne invasion. The 'Fort' on Point Nepean was intended to challenge enemy ships attempting to enter the Bay.

To confuse the enemy further, some of the guns hydraulically 'disappeared' down into the landscape once fired, and were re-loaded underground.

> Large sums of money were spent on the batteries ... Melbourne became one of the best defended ports in the [British] Empire.
> [Major J H Welch, Quarantine Station, Point Nepean, Portsea, Nepean Historical Society, 1968, p.6]

The limestone cliffs at Point Nepean were simple to mine, and many tunnels were dug connecting underground galleries, ammunition storage rooms and the gun emplacements.

While Fort Nepean no longer serves its original purpose, the hidden gun emplacements and connecting underground tunnels are a highlight of a visit to Point Nepean today. Entry is free.

Here's how Bill Tabone of the Australian Paranormal Society described Fort Nepean on Parasearch Radio UK:

> To me it's a really beautiful place during the day ...but when you're there at night, it's eerie. You have these long arched corridors [tunnels] with these little rooms. You've got gun emplacements and ammunition rooms—then there's the ocean itself. The feeling of isolation is pretty powerful!

Bill also reported hearing a series of banging, voices talking, and heavy footsteps from unaccountable sources – but his small group were the only ones present!

But then Bill saw something that stays vividly in his mind to this day:

> We saw shadows moving around in the tunnels. Then I saw a black shadow person, with red eyes, sticking its head around a corner, looking at us! We rushed up there – and there was nothing there! [Bill Tabone, on Parasearch Radio UK, January 2018]

GHOSTS DOWN UNDER

Was the lead researcher of the Australian Paranormal Society 'spooked' by this?

'Not really. Things you see with your own eyes like that, really stand out in your memory! It was probably the most interesting thing of the whole lot that I've seen!' [Bill Tabone, Australian Paranormal Society]

Compare Bill Tabone's experience with that of a local mother, Rebecca Betts from nearby Rye, who took her 3-year-old daughter and the child's two older cousins aged 8 and 10, on a playful excursion to the same tunnels in 2016:

My daughter was super excited to explore the tunnels. Once we were underground and went to the first room, my daughter began panicking and screaming about 'The Man.'

'The Man', it seems, was laughing at her, mocking her—then he started yelling at her!

She quickly wriggled out of my grasp, and instinctively knew her way to a different exit, up a set of stairs. When we reached the surface, my daughter was distraught. [She] has always been highly intuitive, and while I'd like to visit the tunnels again I'm not sure how she would take a further encounter. [Rebecca Betts, Rye, Victoria]

Did Rebecca's daughter see Bill's 'red-eyed shadow person'? We may never know the answer; but having two reliable witnesses certainly suggests that those who guard the Fort Nepean tunnels are still ominously 'active.'

☼

Site details: http://parkweb.vic.gov.au/explore/parks/point-nepean-national-park

5. Showers of Warm Stones

*'The Krakouers huddled in terror inside.
Hundreds of stones must have fallen that night'.*

During the winter months of 1955, visitors and locals flocked to the farming properties of brothers Bill and Doug Hack at Mayanup, Western Australia—some 280 kms (174 miles) south of Perth.

On show there, mostly in the dark hours before midnight, was an on-going, unusual example of the paranormal ... a noisy ghost that terrified inhabitants by pelting warm stones of varying sizes at the homes of two part-aboriginal farm-worker families a mile apart.

> Over the next two years it would baffle and fascinate thousands of people from all walks of life. Many would visit the Shire of Boyup Brook and experience the phenomenon first-hand, while thousands of others would read about the phenomenon in newspapers, books or magazines.
>
> On the evening of 17 May the 'Mayanup stones' had begun to fall. The Nyungar Aboriginal family of Gilbert and Jean Smith were living on Bill and Ethel Hack's sheep and flax-growing property, 'Keninup' with five of their six children in a dwelling about five hundred metres from the main homestead. Jean was pregnant with her seventh child at the time the strange events began. [Helen Hack, The Mystery of the Mayanup Poltergeist, Hesperian, 2000, page 2]

GHOSTS DOWN UNDER

At dusk one night Jean Smith, returning with an armful of wood for the fire, heard a 'plop' as if a stone had forcibly struck the outside wall. Her husband, Gilbert, and several of their children heard the noise, too.

They looked at each other, surprised. Gilbert went outside and walked around their home, seeking the source of the incident. He found nothing unusual and returned to the kitchen table.

Next an old golf ball flew across the room striking the wall, and they also heard the sound of a stone landing on the roof.

A quick discussion followed. The couple felt under attack; was someone trying to scare them? If so, they were succeeding! Gilbert decided they needed immediate help and drove down to the Hack's homestead.

Ethel Hack was in bed, and Bill was away at a meeting. Ethel heard Gilbert yelling to wake up her son Murray who was asleep on the veranda:

> Ethel went outside and confronted Gilbert...assuming he was drunk because he was rambling about being attacked by mysterious stone throwers; she suggested he go home and get some sleep so she and her family could do the same! [Helen Hack, Mayanup Poltergeist, p.4]

Rebuffed by Ethel's dismissal, Gilbert drove his ute to his Nyungar friends, the Krakouers, who lived only three minutes away, directly opposite the 'Keninup' farm entrance.

Molly Krakouer and her husband Alf readily agreed to bundle their seven children up in blankets and spend the rest of the night with Gilbert and Jean.

It was a restless night for both families. Stones continued to fall on the roof or strike the outside walls; the on-going noise made sleep virtually impossible.

One peculiar incident happened inside the home, too. As Molly lay on the floor, 'five large slices of apparently freshly-cut potato' fell on her chest.

Freshly-cut potato? Further weirdnesses followed later.

Just after dawn the four parents made a thorough search around the Smith camp. There were no tracks, no footprints – everything appeared untouched, no sign of intruders, no ready explanations available – just dozens of stones on their roof.

That day, Wednesday 18 May, the Smiths discussed their situation with their boss, Bill Hack. They suggested there had to be a mad man or evil spirit around causing these weird night-time shenanigans. 'Nonsense!' replied Bill. He reckoned some rival Aboriginals were causing the strife. 'If it starts up again, we'll get to the bottom of it!'

During their conversation Bill Hack heard a word he'd never heard before, 'Jannick.' It was one he'd hear time and time again during the 'Mayanup stones' phenomena; it is an Aboriginal word referring to 'a person's spirit'.

Bill decided to drive up to the Smith place that night to check it out for himself. He took his younger brother Ron with him.

Bill drove right around the Smith's camp with his car headlights on high to see if he could catch any culprits in its beams. He saw nothing unusual. As he came to a stop near the front door, he heard a stone rattle on his car roof and reckoned there had to be a practical joker close by.

The brothers went inside and sat in front of the open fire with Jean:

> Ron Hack recalled how he felt his hair stand on end as he witnessed the unexplainable ... he was amazed to see a small stone fly towards him from the rear of the fire, hurtle past his chair and roll along the floor. Almost simultaneously, a lump of charcoal appeared to fall from the ceiling onto the middle of the table. Then Ron heard a rattling sound coming from under the table. He investigated and found a warm stone in an enamel dish ...the Hack brothers were completely at a loss to explain the seemingly unnatural movements of the stones. [Helen Hack, Mayanup Poltergeist, p.7]

During the following day, Bill Hack discussed his reactions with another brother, Doug, who farmed 'Lynford Hill' on the opposite side of the Boyup Brook—Kojonup road to Bill. The three brothers – Bill, Doug and Ron – decided to revisit the Smith camp that evening so Doug could experience the phenomenon for himself.

Once they arrived, Doug didn't have to wait long.

As he entered the Smith's living area, Doug Hack heard a small stone land on the floor behind him. He quickly retraced his steps out the back door hoping to catch any lurking culprit, but there was no one there. Surprised, he went back inside and picked up the stone. It was about the size of a walnut, and quite warm. Doug shook his head, bewildered.

> [Bill] Hack noticed that his three kangaroo dogs and a sheep dog, usually growling and barking at the least sound on the property, remained aloof to the rocks landing on the roof or inside the house.
> [Hugh Schmidt, 'Night Brings Terror to Mayanup', Australasia Post, 1 March 1956, p. 7]

When Bill told other local farmers about these incidents they were sceptical. One even suggested it could have been a possum nesting in a nearby tree that threw the stones. Bill quickly put paid to that – the nearest trees were twenty metres away, too far for a possum to throw anything! 'It must be vandals,' one group of farmers decided.

As well as being blood warm, the stones had other unexpected characteristics: when they landed (on the roof, a table, the floor or on the ground) they never rolled with momentum, they'd just sit there. Further, although it might be wet outside, the stones that landed inside the house were always dry.

> So a few nights later more than twenty farmers surrounded the Smith hut armed with shotguns, rifles, spotlights and lamps to lay the ghost (low).
>
> Just before midnight the stones started to rain down, inside and outside the hut. The farmers shone their lights into the bush about 200 yards/183metres from the hut. They blazed away with their shotguns and rifles – but the stones continued to fall.
>
> They turned the spotlights and rifles up into the trees about 100 yards/91metres from the camp. Still the stones fell. The farmers were shaken by the eerie experience.

The stones fell – or appeared – intermittently until about 4 a.m. None of them fell with much force. Rather they dropped – as if from a height of about one foot/30cm. And how could a practical joker standing in the bush 200 yards/183m. away land stones inside the Smith camp? [Hugh Schmidt, Australasia Post, 1 March 1956, p.8]

Popular storekeeper the late Fred Proctor, who had shops in Boyup Brook and Mayanup, visited the Smith camp having decided to put and end to the 'stones business' because discussion of it frightened some of his lady customers.

Fred and three friends joined a large crowd, including a few newspapermen, around a roaring campfire. Lots of stones fell during their visit, both outside and inside the dwelling, for which they were unable to provide any realistic explanations. Fred's final opinion, reached around midnight, was that the phenomena were supernatural, and he had no hope of stopping it.

The very first newspaper to publish an article on the 'Mayanup stones' was *The Blackwood Times* of Bunbury, W.A. Over a twelve months period *The Blackwood Times* published many news stories from Mayanup and interviewed many of the witnesses.

Their first article, 3rd June 1955, was a front-page interview with Bill Hack in which he put forward his view that the flying stones were not the result of human activity but were of a supernatural origin and defied simple explanation.

Obviously Bill had changed his initial idea of 'rival Aboriginals causing strife' as the basis of the disruptions.

The final paragraph of this item read:

There have been no incidents during the past week and the farmer, and everyone concerned, is hoping that the poltergeist or spirit has decided that he, she or it has had enough fun for the time being.

But the flying stones returned almost immediately, as reported in the following week's paper. A further week later, *The Blackwood Times* carried an interview with Ron and Marjory Hack of 'Lynford Hill' who told of mysterious lights

GHOSTS DOWN UNDER

accompanying some of the stones.

> Strangely enough it was a disbeliever in ghosts, Mrs Bill Hack [Ethel], who had seen them. The sceptical Mrs Hack had decided to wait by a wire fence that runs down a gully about 200 yards/183metres from the hut. She thought she might hear the twang of the wires as an intruder climbed through.
>
> It was about dusk when Mrs Hack saw the light, a small round one suspended in mid-air about 5ft/1.5m from the ground. 'it moved very quickly and very smoothly down the gully, where it disappeared,' Mrs Hack told us, 'there is no road or track where I saw it [eliminating car headlights or their reflections.]' [Hugh Schmidt, Australasia Post, 1 March 1956, p. 8]

Much the same time as this mysterious light was seen by Ethel Hack, her husband called into Gilbert and Jean's place to warn them not to shoot at any figure they saw down near the fence because it would be his wife! While Bill was with the Smiths, three stones landed on the roof and one outside. 'This would be about the same time as the light appeared,' the *Australasian Post* suggested.

The next development, also reported by *The Blackwood Times*, was that the stones had begun raining on Alf and Molly Krakouer's camp on 'Lynford Hill,' in addition to the Smith's dwelling on 'Keninup'.

> The Krakouers were also frightened when the phenomena first began and the white men on the properties were kept busy standing guard with a gun each night. Neighbours now descended on both the Smith's and the Krakouers' camps...
>
> The gatherings at both camps became quite social occasions at a time when many farms were still quite isolated, and many evenings would see a large crowd of visitors gathered around the campfire drinking beer or tea. As many seats as possible were provided around the blazing fire.
>
> Occasionally, a stone would land so gently in a glass of beer that the glass would not break and not a drop would be spilt. Groups of men stood around periodically removing small stones from the rims of their hats. [Helen Hack, Mayanup Poltergeist, pps. 14-15]

At the Krakouers, according to Hugh Schmidt in *Australasia Post*, 'At first the stones started on their camp lightly, but after a week they reached a crescendo and literally rained down':

> One evening they started falling at dark and kept falling until 4 a.m. the following morning. The Krakouers huddled in terror inside. Hundreds of stones must have fallen that night. Meanwhile they continued to fall on the Smith camp.
>
> The remarkable part of the eerie business was that on the Smith property the stones seemed to be centred around Jean Smith. On the Krakouer property they were centred on 14-year-old Audrey Krakouer, the attractive eldest child of the Krakouers. [Australasia Post, 1 March 1956, p. 8]

To establish whether part of this theory was correct, some 'reputable citizens' took Audrey Krakouer away from her home ... the stones continued to fall around her, some as 'big as walnuts.'

Next, a group of six psychic researchers visited Mayanup from Perth. Three of them sat up overnight at the Smiths; the other three at Krakouers. They witnessed stones falling, and heard unusual noises, but couldn't provide any explanations and left.

> They returned again within a couple of weeks and experienced similar poltergeist activity and also reported seeing floating lights. Their final report stated, 'No living person was responsible, but the activity was similar to the poltergeist activity reported from other parts of the world.' [Helen Hack, Mayanup Poltergeist, p. 34]

Earlier, Gilbert Smith had spoken to Bill Hack about bringing an Aboriginal medicine-man or 'Marbar' to Mayanup to help stop the phenomena. Bill was surprised Gilbert held such strong cultural ties with his heritage, but readily agreed.

Old Sammy Miller, who was gifted with the 'sight', came from Mt. Barker with a young carer, and stayed with the Smiths for a few days. Sammy announced a Jannick was the cause of their problems.

All poltergeist activity ceased during his visit, and resumed when he left.

On returning to Mt Barker, Sammy apparently consulted the two other living Marbars in the Great Southern area and they concluded that the Jannick was the spirit of Jean Smith's father, Alf Eades, who was living in the Kojonup area, but seriously ill.

Alf Eades had suffered a stroke while building a fence on Bill Hack's 'Keninup' property before the stones began falling. His granddaughter had found him slumped against a gate and, with help from her father Gilbert, rushed him to Kojonup Hospital. Later discharged, Mr Eades was living with relatives, and disabled by the stroke.

> The witch doctors believed that because Jean was Alf Eades' favourite child, his spirit was leaving his body and travelling all the way from Kojonup [60km] to the Smith's camp at 'Keninup' to be with her... the witch-doctors said that Alf Eades's spirit needed to be put back into his body and agreed to do this. [Helen Hack, Mayanup Poltergeist, pps. 40-41]

The 'Ghost Laying Ceremony' at Kojonup, held on 5 July 1955, attracted a large, respectful crowd. Bill and Doug Hack accepted the invitation to attend, as well as most members of Mr Eades' extended family.

There was a large group of interested bystanders gathered at Gilbert and Jean Smith's place on 'Keninup' for the duration of the distant ceremony, too.

> The ceremony took place in the evening gloom around the humpy in which the ailing Alf Eades lay sleeping most of the time. He did rouse himself once though, to declare emphatically, 'My spirit never left me! Go away you bloody witch-doctors!' [Helen Hack, Mayanup Poltergeist, p. 41]

The old man, it seems, had been brought up in the white man's ways; he lacked a traditional Nyungar upbringing. The notion of 'witch-doctors' was foreign to him; but the ceremony went ahead despite his feeble protest.

> The witch-doctors had apparently worked out a plan of action. Sammy Miller, all sanguine and business-like, took up station at the head of Alf Eade's bed and faced in the direction of Mayanup...
>
> Freddie Winmar took a blanket down into a hollow behind Alf Eade's camp. He went alone, but in the light of the full moon he could be seen crouching over the blanket. The natives watched

spellbound as Freddie rose shakily from the ground holding the blanket as if he had something under it.

> Muttering in hoarse, guttural tones, he carefully carried his 'burden' up the hill towards the hessian camp ...Inside the camp he drew the blankets from Alf Eade's body, took the spirit from under the blanket and put it back into his body ...ostensibly reintroduced the wandering spirit into the native's body. [Hugh Schmidt, Australasia Post, 1 March 1956, p. 32]

Alf Eades is reported to have said, 'It felt just like a big gust of wind hitting me in the chest.'

Would this be the end of the stone-throwing? No, far from it!

Those waiting at 'Keninup' for the visiting party to return home from the ceremony heard two stones land on the Smith's roof. As the Smith family drove up the driveway, they were showered in stones as well.

Six weeks after the ceremony, Alf Eade died.

The stones continued falling during the next ten weeks, and gradually weakened. On 20 September 1955 only two stones fell during daylight; then it was quiet for months.

In April 1956 – almost a year since it first began – it started all over again with bigger stones, bottles, boots and bones. On 20 August 1956 there was a truly spectacular poltergeist session which Bill Hack recorded in his diary:

> 5.30p.m. I fluked a most extraordinary session. It was broad daylight ... a brick on the roof, brass tap from kero drum hit wall from SW. Tried to calculate velocity by throwing it back at the wall. Each time I threw I was hit in back by a one or two pound [1kg] stone. I challenged the thrower to continue. Every time for 25 times he responded. The he dropped a cake of soap in front of us. Then a child's shoe hit me. Another cake of soap hit wall. It was replaced on table. It immediately hit one on the back. It was replaced and so on. Then followed forks, spoons. a file, onion, knife, socks, ball of silver paper and potatoes. The kitchen utensils, soap etc did not travel more than eight to fifteen feet [4½m]. The original brass tap I left lying on the ground and walked towards the car. The tap hit me on the back. No one was within 10ft [3m] of it. Then a stone weighing 35 pounds [16kg]

known to have been in the fireplace fell gently on to the tank.
[Helen Hack, Mayanup Poltergeist, p. 45]

A few months later, the Krakouer family decided they'd had enough. They left Doug Hack's employment and moved to the Mount Barker district.

About six months later, on 26 May 1957, Gilbert and Jean Smith made a similar decision – they had stayed on through the whole ruckus because of their rapport with Bill Hack. The Jannick and the constant visitors wore them out; the family camped near the Mayanup Racecourse for the first few weeks. The mysterious landing there of a lemonade bottle on their water tank, followed by stones and sticks, was enough to make them move away the following morning.

Months later, Gilbert and Jean called in to visit Bill and Ethel Hack, and Bill persuaded them to visit their old dwelling:

> As they drove up to it and opened the car door, one stone landed on the roof followed by a shower of small stones. Then came more showers of stones, one bottle, one milk tin, one piece of bone and one stick ...
>
> The Smiths called in again on August 10th ... went up to the abandoned camp and in a few minutes one bottle, various stones, an empty match box and a cigarette butt were collected as they fell to the ground, some inside the house and some outside. [Helen Hack, Mayanup Poltergeist, p. 61]

The Smiths moved into their own home in Boyup Brook in 1964, and Gilbert died the following year, a relatively young man.

Their former home, on the hill at 'Keninup' where it all started, collapsed after twenty years of being vacant and was subsequently demolished.

Jean Smith was asked if she still had the Jannick calling at her home on the outskirts of Boyup Brook after all these years.

'Yes,' she replied, 'I just don't tell anyone any more.'

☼

6. Solomon Wiseman's Wisdom

At night a shadowy form rose from an old vault in the garden

In June 1821, the wife of former convict Solomon Wiseman, mother of his six children died suddenly. Her body was interred in a vault behind the family residence.

An accident? An illness? Or was she murdered?

Whatever the cause, Jane Wiseman wasn't ready to leave. She lingered around their home, Cobham Hall, long after her death. Many insist she is still there.

Does she seek revenge?

The great-great-great-grandfather of the acclaimed Australian writer, Kate Greville, Solomon Wiseman made the voyage to the colony in 1806 as a convicted felon, charged with stealing timber from his employer's boat. He was sentenced to death, but because he had sailed British Government spies across the English Channel to France, his death sentence was commuted to 'transportation for life.'

As a further concession, Solomon Wiseman was able to take his wife, Jane, and three children to New South Wales with him.

Jane Wiseman, being a free woman, applied to have her husband assigned to her as a convict servant and the authorities agreed. Less than a year after being sentenced Solomon was, effectively, a free man and able to devote himself to making his fortune.

On his wife's recommendation he soon had a ticket-of-leave and a year after that a full pardon. [Richard Davis, Great Australian Ghost Stories, Sydney, 2012, pps. 78-79]

Once free of his shackles, Wiseman did very well. He purchased a sloop and worked as a coastal trader, eventually moving his family onto their own land on the Hawkesbury River, 60km (37 miles) north-west of Sydney in 1819. He erected a dwelling near the river bank, and commenced farming

It must have been a difficult life for Jane, raising (by now) six children on the edge of civilization, growing and harvesting corn for sustenance, devoid of female companionship. Her husband may not have been the most congenial company, as he was known to be strict and overbearing, at least with his assigned convict servants.

In fact, he was probably responsible for creating at least one Hawkesbury haunting:

> The story goes that a young convict, anxious to see his sweetheart in Sydney, begged Wiseman to give him a permit [to travel]. This the 'Governor' [Wiseman] refused and instead put him under a cruel taskmaster who had him chained to a roadmaking gang. He attempted to escape by swimming the river, but his leg-irons hampered him and he was drowned.

> For years the ghost of the young boy was supposed to come to the house and the clank, clank of his chains sent a shiver down the spine of travelers who claim to have heard it. [Windsor and Richmond Gazette, 'Shadowy Forms at Wiseman's', 27 January 1928]

It was two years after settling at Hawkesbury, and before completing their rather-pretentious, sandstone home, *Cobham Hall,* that Jane died.

As a child, Kate Grenville heard stories of her ancestors and wrote:

> The best bit of the story, as far as I was concerned, was the part about his wife, Jane. Wiseman was supposed to have killed her by throwing her down the stairs of the house he'd built on the

Hawkesbury. Her ghost was rumored to haunt it. – Kate Grenville (as a ten-year-old)

Here's a more recent comment on Jane Wiseman's death:

> Possibly the most heinous of Wiseman's sins, however, has never been proven – the alleged murder of his wife, Jane. According to his great-great-great-granddaughter, famous novelist Kate Grenville, family legend has it that Jane was thrown to her death off the balcony at Cobham Hall after a heated argument, cracking her head on the bottom step. [Miller & Osborn, Sydney, 2010, p. 115]

Shortly after Jane's death, a shadowy form began to appear at night. It rose from an old vault in the garden and made its way towards the house. Many believed it was Jane trying to draw attention to a treasure she had hidden in her bedroom.

> Several years after the ghost was last seen a box of sovereigns was found under the floor of the old room. [Windsor and Richmond Gazette, 'Shadowy Forms at Wiseman's', 27 January 1928]

Solomon Wiseman wasn't frightened of ghosts! He pressed on with his vision of a ferry across the Hawkesbury.

> ...he was given a lease of what became known as Wiseman's Ferry on the Hawkesbury River on condition that government horses and property were carried on it free of charge [Vivienne Parsons, Australia Dictionary of Biography, Vol. 2, Melbourne, 1976]

He then received further land grants, built an inn on one bank and obtained a liquor license for it. Solomon Wiseman died a rich man in 1838, and was buried beside his first wife, Jane.

However, the legend of the Hawkesbury ghost – or should it be ghosts? – remains. There's the tale of a swagman who camped at the old house after Jane's death and awoke to the choked screams of a woman. He then heard a door slam and sat up to listen as footsteps echoed along the stone corridor and a shadowy form flitted past him.

When this was followed by the clanking of leg irons approaching his room – probably the love-sick young convict—the swagman 'grabbed his 'matilda' and fled out another door.

And who could blame him?

Today, many visitors to the old house – which is now a fancy hotel – report having observed a woman in a long gown hurrying through the rooms and corridors, or insist they heard the swish-swish of a silky dress, a scraping of feet, a gasping cry.

The ferry that bears Solomon Wiseman's name still operates to this day, and according to Hawkesbury's own website, the settlement of Wiseman's Ferry ...

> ... is a favorite retreat for Sydney-siders... its popularity has neither eroded its rural charm nor disturbed the hotel's famous ghost.

7. He Being Dead, Yet Speaketh

Foul smells ...and an apparition of a large, bearded man threatening unwanted visitors.

Situated about 100kms (62 Miles) by road south-east of Hobart, Port Arthur is the best preserved penal settlement in Australia. It was named after George Arthur, the Lt.-Governor of the Van Diemen's Land which is now known as the island state, Tasmania.

> ...shiploads of convicts – men, women and children – were transported here from England for crimes which could be as petty as stealing a loaf of bread. . [Dr. Maurice Marsh, 'Haunted' – 1989 TV documentary series]

Well over one thousand prisoners died at Port Arthur during its brutal 47-year history as a penal colony in the mid to late 1800's, many of them as a result of flogging, starvation, murder, suicide, attempted escape and hanging. Of the 1,646 graves on the off-shore Island of the Dead, only those of staff and military personnel are marked.

The rest have been condemned to anonymity for eternity.

At Port Arthur, these prisoners were often treated to the most inhuman treatment imaginable, chained for weeks at a time, forbidden to speak, or even hanged for their misdemeanours. [Dr. Maurice Marsh, 'Haunted' – 1989 TV documentary series]

Boys as young as 9 were used for hard labor. Solitary confinement cells in the Separate Prison building inflicted mental punishment in place of floggings and as a result, many developed mental illnesses from the lack of light and sound.

Port Arthur was not a happy place! It's hardly surprising that ghostly occurrences have been reported at the site since 1870, but what is surprising is that the earliest of these were not necessarily the anguished ghosts of earthbound convicts!

In 1842 the Colonial Secretary in London authorized the building of *'The Parsonage'* at Port Arthur. It was a double-storied building intended perhaps to indicate the senior status of the clergyman in their midst.

The Reverend George Eastman was chaplain from 1855 to 1870. A large, convivial man, he was known amongst the convicts as the 'Good Parson'. It is recorded that when a convict's time had expired, Rev George Eastman always had some money to help them on their way.

In April 1870, Eastman was unwell in bed at *'The Parsonage'* when a call came through for him to attend a dying prisoner at a distant outstation. Putting duty before his own health, he visited the man, but caught a chill in the process, which developed into pneumonia. He died two days later, aged 48 years.

> When the Reverend George Eastman, a man of enormous girth, died in an upstairs bedroom [of 'The Parsonage'] his empty coffin was manoeuvred up the narrow stairs but, when filled, it was found to be too heavy to be brought out the same way.

A rope was rigged to lower the coffin from the bedroom window to the ground, but halfway down the rope snapped, the coffin fell and the bloated corpse of the late, lamented clergyman tumbled into the garden. [Richard Davis, Great Australian Ghost Stories, Sydney, 2012, pps 185-186]

His funeral service was followed by a long procession through the settlement, according to the Hobart newspaper *The Mercury*, to the wharf where six boats awaited to convey the mourners who desired to follow the remains to the 'Isle of the Dead', where the body was interred in a new vault.

It seems that George Eastman, even in death, had discovered another way to influence the residents of Port Arthur! The inscription on his headstone on the 'Isle of the Dead' reads: 'He being Dead yet Speaketh' (Hebrews, 11-4).

Almost immediately, strange incidents began to occur. Eastman's replacement—the Rev. Haywood—and his wife witnessed a number of eerie activities in their new home.

The best-known descriptions of *'The Parsonage'* manifestations were published in a series of articles in the now long-defunct Hobart newspaper, *The Clipper*. Their author was George Grunsell, a regular visitor from Hobart who stayed with the Haywoods when calling at Port Arthur. One incident he recalls occurred when Reverend Haywood's wife and children were due to return to Port Arthur after a short stay in Hobart:

> ... the doctor – McCarthy by name I believe—seeing the lights shining from various upstairs rooms in 'The Parsonage' concluded that the Haywood family had arrived from Hobart. He accordingly paid a visit to welcome them on their return, and rang the front bell for admission.
>
> Mr Haywood opened the door and the doctor made known the cause of his visit. Mr Haywood informed the doctor that they had no arrived yet...'Not arrived!' said the doctor, 'I made sure they had come, and seeing the lights upstairs concluded Mrs Haywood was busy putting things in order.'
>
> Mr Haywood stared at him in astonishment, and assured the doctor he must be mistaken, as there were only the servant and himself in the house, and they were both in the kitchen at the back, and had not ever been upstairs, therefore there could have been no lights.

The doctor being positive, they both made an inspection of the rooms, but found them all in darkness. ['Port Arthur Twenty Years Ago', The Clipper, 19 August 1893, p. 4]

While this may not be an outstanding example of 'spirit manifestation', George Grunsell assured his readers that 'others in the settlement had seen the lights' as well as the doctor, and 'they were a subject of speculation during the following day.'

Remember too, in those days it was hardly a matter of a forgotten electric light switch, rather each wick had to be ignited by hand to produce light.

Further incidents of inexplicable light followed:

One evening Mr and Mrs Haywood were sitting in the drawing room upstairs. The door was open. Suddenly they were struck by the appearance of a most intense light, which streamed from under the door of a room on the opposite side of the landing. The room was used as a study.

Creeping cautiously up, Mr Haywood peeped through the keyhole, and to his astonishment could see the interior as though brilliantly lighted up with gas. He turned the handle and opened the door, when lo and behold! all was in sudden darkness again. [The Clipper, 19 August 1893, p. 4]

The next instance happened several months later – this time with independent, reliable witnesses. Sir Valentine and Lady Flemming were staying at *'The Parsonage'* and the subject of the 'mysterious lights' was discussed.

Sir Valentine, a Judge, was, as visitor Grunsell described him, 'too old a stager and too matter-of-fact' to believe there was anything so uncanny, and laughed off the whole affair. But he was soon to change his attitude:

The lights appeared again exactly as on the previous occasion. They peeped through the keyhole; they opened the door, but to no purpose – the result was the same as before. Sir Valentine gravely shook his head and suggested a thorough examination of the premises by daylight.

Accordingly, with the doctor's assistance, an investigation took place, but nothing would account for the lights. [The Clipper, 19 August 1893, p. 4]

On another occasion, Mrs Haywood had a puzzling experience. It was her habit to go around *'The Parsonage'* every night before retiring to ensure that all doors and windows were safely locked and barred against intruders:

> On descending early one morning to let the manservant in from the penitentiary, she was amazed to find a candle burning in a candlestick on a chair in the middle of the kitchen…

> Who lit the candle or how it got there remained a mystery. Had it been burning all night it would have burnt out; besides Mrs Haywood was quite certain it was not there when she locked up.
> [The Clipper, 26 August 1893, p. 4]

Perhaps 'The Good Parson' was merely attempting to shed much-needed light on the colony, but a few years later, another – and this time, a less benevolent spirit – would begin to pay regular visits to the parsonage.

Julie Miller & Grant Osborn relate that there were also occurrences of ….

> … foul smells …and an apparition of a large bearded man threatening unwanted visitors. [Miller & Osborn, Something is Out There, Sydney, 2010, p.46]

At one time, the Roman Catholic chaplain was called away, leaving his sister alone in their home. Rev. Haywood and his wife invited her to be a guest at *'The Parsonage'* during her brother's absence. She gladly accepted, blissfully unaware of the terror she would soon experience.

The lady was made comfortable in the guest bedroom on the ground floor, a front room on the right of the main entrance of *'The Parsonage'*. She had not been there many days when the Haywoods – sleeping upstairs – heard loud knocking and banging from the ground floor:

> Presently they heard a piercing scream, and a moment afterwards their lady friend rushed up the stairs in the greatest terror and burst into their bedroom. Having struck a light and pacified her to some extent, they learned that she was awakened by a knocking sound in her room.

> Thinking it to be rats in the skirting, she reached out and shied her boots about without effect. Presently it seemed to be all over the floor and under her bed … She was so worked up that she could

> stand it no longer, and letting out a scream rushed up into Mrs Haywood's bedroom …She declared she heard the patter of feet following her upstairs. [The Clipper, 19 August 1893, p. 4]

As their visitor was too frightened to return downstairs to her bed, a shakedown was made for her in the study – 'the room in which the lights had appeared a few years earlier.' Rev. Haywood did not go downstairs to check on the source of the knocking, but contented himself by looking over the banisters before retiring to his room, closing the door firmly. 'This was no sooner done,' Grunsell wrote, 'than 'rap, rap' was heard upon the same [door] on the outside. He at once opened it, and found darkness; only that and nothing more.'

The next 'manifestation' was particularly startling, especially for the maid who experienced it.

The guest bedroom (from where the chaplain's sister fled) had remained unoccupied for some time. One Saturday after the maid scrubbed the floor, she lit a fire to dry the room and freshen the air. After dark she returned to check the fire.

Suddenly, she let out a spine-chilling shriek and fell to the floor, senseless.

> The Haywoods rushed in, and endeavoured by all means in their power – smelling salts, cold water, burnt feathers, etc. – to restore her to consciousness, but in vain. As a last resort, Rev. Haywood placed her head between his knees and soundly boxed her ears.

> This brought her round, but it was some time before the girl was sufficiently calm to explain what happened. At last she did, when she declared that on entering the room she distinctly saw the figure of a man in a peculiar garment, looking at her through the window, and grasping in his hand a knife or dagger, which he held as though about to strike. [The Clipper, 19 August 1893, p. 4]

Grasping a knife or dagger? This was certainly not 'The Good Parson' returning to bring joy and goodwill to the colony!

George Grunsell commented that ever afterwards the maid refused to enter that room again after dark. Hardly surprising!

The room became known by the family, Grunsell wrote, as the 'haunted room.' It was placed at Grunsell's disposal during one of his visits, but he denies being disturbed by any apparitions while staying there.

However, Grunsell did share one unusual experience with Rev. Haywood one evening while descending the stairs in the dark, he recalled:

> 'I was about two stairs behind him, and we both had our hands on the banister. All at once he stopped and called out 'Is that you, Martie?' (Martie was his eldest son, 12 years.) Receiving no reply he asked again with a like result He then called for a light to be brought, and although we searched not a soul was near. He declared that he most distinctly felt a hand placed upon his on the banister and again withdrawn. He thought it was his boy playing him a trick in the dark. But it was not so... [The Clipper, 26 August 1893, p. 4]

The final *'Parsonage'* incident during the Haywood's residency occurred one night when George Grunsell was guesting in the 'haunted room' downstairs, the family were also entertaining Mrs Haywood's mother and sister (Mrs and Miss Price) who were occupying a large room with two windows upstairs, shared with one of the young Haywood children.

'Mrs Price was a very strong-minded lady,' Grunsell emphasised while recounting this story. 'She had seen far too much to cause her to be easily frightened.'

> On one particular night [during her visit] Mrs Price was unable to sleep. She lay with her eyes open. The moon was shining and with its dim light just made the interior of the room visible to her sight.
>
> Suddenly she became conscious that somebody had entered her room, and glancing towards the door beheld a human figure draped in white. Her first thought was to make a move or to speak, but it struck her that the intruder might be a burglar in disguise intent upon robbing her ...and to attract attention to herself might possibly mean something serious against her life.
>
> She therefore lay motionless, but with half open eyes followed the movements of the supposed burglar. The mysterious figure having entered the room went through the motion of striking a match upon the wall, and immediately afterwards there was the

appearance of light as from a Lucifer [a self-igniting match].

> This done, it then made its way round the foot of the bed to a cot in which one of the children slept. For a moment it stood looking at the sleeping child, then turning round glided silently out of the room and was gone. [The Clipper, 26 August 1893, p. 4]

Mrs Price told of her experience next morning, which 'caused no end of speculation as to who or what the ghost might be.'

The Haywoods and their guests were probably the first people to see ghosts at *'The Parsonage'*. But they would certainly not be the last!

Soon after these experiences took place, Port Arthur closed as a penal colony (in 1877). Some surrounding land was auctioned off, and the last of the convicts were sent elsewhere. The Haywoods moved away; and *The Parsonage* became privately owned. An era had finished.

Then the bushfires of 1895 and 1897 ravaged the Tasman Peninsula, and destroyed a number of Port Arthur buildings. *The Parsonage* was badly damaged and later remodeled as a single-storey structure.

But the ghostly story of *'The Parsonage'* was far from over!

The heritage supervisor during the restoration of the Port Arthur site in the 1980s, tells an interesting tale:

> ... a group of tradesmen staying in 'The Parsonage' while doing renovations were driven from the building after a terrifying night of strange and seemingly supernatural events, including unexplained bangs and bumps and one tradesman being pinned down on his bed by an invisible entity.
>
> Another worker reported seeing a woman dressed in white who was accompanied by a sudden drop in temperature and billowing curtains. [J G Montgomery, Haunted Australia: Ghosts of the Great South Land, Pennsylvania, 2016, p.225]

Could the 'woman in white' be the same apparition seen by Mrs. Price over a century earlier, the one who had ...

> 'made its way round the foot of the bed to a cot in which one of the children slept. For a moment it stood looking at the sleeping child.'

If so, then she appears to be a peaceful and loving soul. Perhaps she lost a child and endlessly searches for it, or maybe she was a convict and therefore denied the opportunity to have children of her own, so now delights in watching over others.

The woman in white might even be the young bride of the accountant, who lived next door to the Parsonage. According to letters inherited by descendents of the English side of her family, the young woman felt intimidated and restricted at Port Arthur and found comfort in her friendship with her neighbor, the Parson's wife.

Sadly, the young woman died while giving birth to a stillborn child, and her unbaptized infant was buried in the Parsonage gardens.

The letters she had written to family at 'home' were kept safe and handed down through many generations. Eventually, they came into the possession of a couple who visited Australia and were hoping to fill in some gaps in the family tree.

According to Peter Richman, producer of the 2003 documentary Ghosts of Port Arthur, during a visit to Port Arthur, the couple ...

> ...walked past the Parsonage one afternoon and took a photo of the building, and when it was developed, they found an image of the baby, clearly visible in the left [corner]—so perhaps he and his mother are still searching for one another?

The woman in white is not the only one to frequent the Parsonage. Over the years since the original occurrences in 1870, manifestations at *The Parsonage* have become increasingly violent.

> These days, no one spends the night in the Parson's House. Laughter and footsteps seem harmless enough, but there is something eerie about the old house at night. It is as though locked windows and closed doors hold back a host of unhappy demons. [B & J Emberg, Ghostly Tales of Tasmania, Launceston, 1991, p.123]

☼

8. Bridge over Haunted Waters

*Neither whip nor spur would induce their horses
to cross the bridge.*

In Wollongong, New South Wales, there once stood a bridge which today is buried under the Princes Highway where it crosses the freeway. A sign on the freeway overpass still indicates that this was the site of Ghost Creek Bridge.

Why was it so-named?

Our story begins one fateful evening in 1836, when Lieutenant Henry Otway dined with his boss Colonel Leahy, and apparently had a few too many glasses of wine.

Otway was in charge of a stockade in Wollongong, New South Wales, where a handful of soldiers were stationed to supervise convict labor brought to the site to erect a bridge.

> When he returned to the stockade, the sentry challenged him, but instead of replying and giving the password, he seized the sentry and attempted to take his musket from him. The sentry then allowed Lieutenant Otway to pass to his quarters inside the camp, but afterwards reported the occurrence to the sergeant who relieved him. [Alexander Steward, Reminiscences of Illawarra, Wollongong 1984, p.24]

Lieutenant Otway sobered up overnight and realized the matter had been reported. In his sober state, he knew, without doubt, that he would have to face a court martial. This would mean suffering the indignity of having his sword broken and being dismissed from the Army in disgrace.

He had no choice.

> On 7 April 1836, Lt. Otway held his prayer book in one hand and a pistol in the other and took his own life. [Illawarra Mercury.internet site]

Even before the news of Otway's death was known, several locals insist they saw him standing on the bridge, waving a greeting. He then faded away before their eyes!

According to Balgownie historian Carol Herben: 'For the next forty years or so, Lieutenant Otway was blamed for the manner in which humans and animals became spooked when traveling that stretch of road late at night.'

> In those days many local residents would not travel down the hill after nightfall, for fear they would meet the ghost. On one occasion, three gentlemen who had been attending a meeting in Wollongong were returning to their homes south of Wollongong late at night on horseback.
>
> When they reached the 'Ghost Bridge', neither whip nor spur would induce their horses to cross the bridge. The fears of the horses were soon transmitted to their riders ...they spent the night at Wollongong, returning home in the early morning. [A. E. Organ, 'The Early Days', Illawarra Mercury, 17 September 1920, p.1]

One might understand why Otway was reluctant to leave. No doubt he regretted his drunken folly which caused him such desperation that he felt it necessary to take his own life. But was there another ghost – this one on horseback— also spooking the residents in that area of Wollongong?

Albert Elias Organ (author of *The Early Days*, 1920) lived in the area as a child, and tells of one night when he was sitting with his father and neighbor Rev. Mr. Kingdom.

> ...we have distinctly heard a horse galloping up the road. The sound started at the bridge and continued up to the top of the hill, where it would cease, only to at once recommence at the bridge. This would be repeated several times.

Surprisingly, this incident did not phase the reverend,

who then proceeded to share his own experiences of the mysterious ghost rider:

> [he] ... told us on one occasion he was sitting on the verandah on a moonlight night when he heard the sounds of a horse galloping from the bridge, and a horse with a man on its back rode up to his gate, then instantly disappeared.
>
> On another occasion, he was returning from Mount Keira in company with his wife on a moonlit night when they saw a horse and rider in front of them, which suddenly disappeared through a three-railed fence on Mr. Stewart's road boundary, where neither slip rails or gate existed. [A. E. Organ, Illawarra Mercury, 17 September 1920, p.1]

Was Lieutenant Otway now haunting the area on a ghost horse, or was this another specter entirely? We may never know. What we do know is that there are two creeks in Wollongong with interesting names.

We have Ghost Creek – where Otway supervised convicts to build a bridge.

And then, just a few kilometers away, there is Haunted Creek.

We can only wonder what stories Haunted Creek may be hiding in its murky depths.

9. Dead Mailman calls for 'Help'

'Teddy light belongs spirit o' mailman wanna talk you'

Almost a hundred years ago, a fatality occurred close to Blairmore cattle station homestead in Queensland.

After a sulky accident a companion left an injured mailman sitting near a tree while he went for help. A fierce electric storm had broken, and the mailman left the tree and staggered towards the station. In a weak condition he either collapsed and fell, or was struck by lightning.

> The injured mailman was found lying face down in a pool of water near Sandy Creek, about three miles from the homestead. When help arrived from Blairmore, his dead body was taken to the homestead ... [Geoff Thursby, Courier Mail, Brisbane, 24 December 1946, p.2]

Geoff Thursby, who wrote this article for the Courier Mail, grew up on Blairmore Station. 'The incident', he wrote, 'happened on Christmas Eve, more than 25 years ago.' That places the date of the fatality as some time before 1921.

> The next day he [the mailman] was buried on a creek bank about half a mile [800m] from the station. Because rigor mortis* had not set in, the station aborigines said the man was not dead, and that he would become a 'debil-debil.' [Geoff Thursby, Courier Mail]   *rigor mortis: the stiffening of a body after death.

The 'Blairmore Light' was first seen the very next night. Perhaps the aboriginal prophecy had come true.

> One Christmas Eve in the 1930s the 'spirit' was responsible for a mass aboriginal walkout from the station. The aborigines were all camped in a hut about 300 yards [275 meters] from the station ... the light appeared not more than 100 yards [91 meters] from the hut. Early on Christmas morning the aborigines had gone. [Geoff Thursby, Courier Mail]

The 'Blairmore Light' remains a mystery to this day. Many people have followed it, hoping to find some kind of explanation for it. All have failed.

Geoff Thursby claims there's only one man, un-named, who followed the Light into a nearby swamp and refused to discuss the incident. Thursby says 'A mention of it brings a tight-lipped silence from him.'

Thursby claims to have seen the Light often, but he still awaits a convincing explanation of its appearance. He also stated the incident and its aftermath became 'part of my life and not something to fear'.

Ted O'Brien, who worked on Blairmore for more than 25 years, is conversant with the Light's full history. He has tried to chase it many times – on foot, on horseback and by car.

> Just when a pursuer thinks he is closing in on the Light to gain its secret, his attention is mysteriously distracted. When he looks again, the Light has gone. It immediately re-appears behind him.
>
> Spirit-like, it remains stationary until its pursuer again almost reaches it. The same unfathomable momentary distraction occurs and the Light vanishes. Seconds later it re-appears. One night Mr O'Brien got within less than fifty yards [46 meters] of the Light.
> [Frank Cusack, Australian Ghost Stories, Melbourne, 1967, p.79]

Geoff Thursby retold one of Ted O'Brien's accounts of chasing the Light: 'The glowing fireball remained steadily in front of him. Then Mr O'Brien tripped and fell heavily. Falling, he heard what he described as a noise like a bullock jumping over an embankment into a creek bed. As he regained his feet he peered into the darkness. The 'Light' had vanished.

O'Brien told Thursby: 'No one will ever tell me that there wasn't something different about the Light that night.'

The next day when he told Aboriginals about what had happened, one of them paled and said in a husky voice: 'Teddy light belongs spirit o' mailman wanna talk you.'

Thirteen years before Geoff Thursby's article was published, the Smith's Weekly in Sydney made a reference to the Blairmore Light:

> The appearance of something alleged to be a supernatural phenomenon is scaring the entire population of Blairmore district, in Central Burnett, Queensland.
>
> Frequently at night, residents see a light about the height of a man from the ground, which moves slowly, they say, across the flats towards Bandera Creek, where it disappears...
>
> Some of the bolder residents have at times chased it, but without discovering what it is; and on occasion some of these brave spirits have fired shots at it, without result. It remains as much a mystery as ever.
>
> Various theories have been put forward to account for the 'ghost', but nobody is satisfied.
>
> The aborigines in the district decline to accept any theory. They maintain that it is a ghost, and declare that the visitation is a precursor of misfortune... [Smith's Weekly, 23 September 1933, p.5]

A precursor of misfortune? It's likely Jim Matheson would agree with that!

Matheson was a returned World War One digger, and a Justice of the Peace. For many years he had been a Government Stock Inspector stationed at Mt Isa, then Cracow, and later at Gayndah (close by Blairmore). Eventually he became a Brisbane City councilor.

In 1957 details of Jim Matheson's brush with the 'Blairmore Light' were released:

> Matheson was driving along the boundary road of Blairmore station on a humid, stormy night when his car became bogged in a wide patch of mud. Unable to free the car, Matheson settled down in the back seat to sleep until morning.

Minutes later another car came along the road traveling fast and, before Matheson could give warning, ploughed into the mud up to its axles. The second car contained a commercial traveler and his wife. The three chatted for a while then returned to their cars to sleep.

Just prior to dozing off, Jim Matheson heard urgent cries of 'Help! Help! Help!' He climbed out of his car and tried to work out where the calls came from. He realized they were from the middle of a nearby paddock. He quickly pulled on his boots, and strode off in the directions of distress calls, which were continuing.

Before he had gone ten paces Matheson recalls there was 'half a stone' [3kgs] of sticky black mud clinging to each of his boots, but he struggled on.

Then he saw the flickering light. It wasn't any shape you could put a name to; it swirled and changed, swelled and shrank, like a formless, luminous blob of jelly.

As he moved towards the Light, it seemed to be heading in his direction, and the cries for help grew louder. Suddenly, the cries...

... seemed to be all around him, and inside him, coming not from his throat but through the pores of his skin! The terrified man couldn't move any further, he couldn't think! He felt as though he was in the grip of some deadly struggle and that something dead was robbing him of his own life force.

Then, mercifully, another sound intruded on his consciousness – the sound of the commercial traveler's wife screaming.

Instinct to go to the aid of a woman in distress made Matheson turn and run back to the cars. He believes his life was saved at that moment.

Quickly, the three travelers gathered some sticks, and using a little petrol, started a fire. They huddled around its cheerful glow for the remainder of the night, hearing the distant cries of 'Help! Help!' being carried to their ears on the wind. As dawn approached the sound faded and finally could no longer be heard.

Jim Matheson searched the paddock in daylight but could find nothing remarkable.

Burnett District, Queensland

Later he related his experience to a local cattleman.

'You were lucky,' the cattleman said, 'A stockman once heard the ghost crying for help and went to it. He was dead when they found him and his face was not a pretty sight. Some people believe his spirit took the original ghost's place and that the stockman has been trying to catch another victim ever since. It could have been you out there tonight, Jim, crying for help.'

☼

[Privately owned]

10. Hostess with the Ghostess

The clerks saw, to their astonishment, an old lady, white-haired, small in build, mount the stairs.

Three houses figured prominently in the Brookes families lives, each of them the scene of lavish entertainment.

Two of them had a resident ghost!

When eighteen-year-old Mabel Emmerton, daughter of Melbourne's leading society hostess, announced her engagement to Australian tennis ace Norman Brookes in 1908, many expressed surprise. He was almost thirteen years older than her.

> He was dour, she ebullient; both very competitive, ambitious, and determined. They were married with some splendor, in St Paul's Anglican Cathedral, Melbourne, on 19 April 1911. [J.R. Poynter, Australian Dictionary of Biography, Vol.13, M.U. P., 1993]

Norman and Mabel settled in a large house opposite *Raveloe* – Mabel's childhood home in the elite Melbourne suburb of South Yarra – and a few years later also purchased *Cliff House* as a holiday home in the bayside township of Mt.Eliza.

> We first saw Cliff House in a thunderstorm ... the agent was busy selling the surroundings and cast a contemptuous glance at the house, saying 'Of course, it must come down; it is riddled with

white ants, also the roof is half gone and there is no water laid on; don't consider the house in the purchase, but the land ...' [Dame Mabel Brookes, Crowded Galleries, (London, 1956), p.108]

They purchased the property the next day. Mabel had fallen in love with the house, despite its shortcomings. She flatly refused to have it demolished. 'It had been a home for so long, about eighty years,' she later recollected, adding 'people had left behind in it the faint echo of their happiness.' So they patched it up, added extensions including a second storey, a servant's cottage and a gardener's cottage, and landscaped the extensive gardens.

We can only wonder what the other resident of the house thought about this. Thirty years later, Mabel wrote:

> Cliff House once had a [ghostly] visitor; when we bought the old home and made it habitable, the children often spoke of footsteps, coming from the beach to the back of the kitchen. The maids declared, too, they had heard footfalls – a measured walk of an old man passing by their windows and up the drive: and one night I heard them myself. [Dame Mabel Brookes, Crowded Galleries, London, 1956, p.275]

Once the renovations were completed in 1927, the Brookes held a garden party at Cliff House in honor of the tennis champions from several Australian States. The elite of Australian society at the time – including the Governor-General, Lord Stonehaven – mingled with distinguished tennis players, and all admired the garden and magnificent views.

When the guests had departed, Lord Stonehaven and his wife remained, having been invited to stay overnight.

That evening, after the Stonehavens had retired, another Cliff House 'special' visitor made an appearance:

> Viscountess Stonehaven, wife of the Governor-General, our guest, saw him standing near her window, or rather she saw his feet and legs. She called out, but when I turned on the garden floodlights there was nothing. [Dame Mabel Brookes, Crowded Galleries, London, 1956, p.275]

Mabel Brookes was never disturbed by these unexpected appearances and initially dismissed them as local fishermen walking to and from their boats tied up in a sheltered cove at the base of the cliff. The long driveway to the house followed a track used for years for that very purpose.

As time passed, however, she began to wonder if there was, perhaps, another explanation for the mysterious footsteps.

In her 1956 autobiography, [the now Dame] Mabel Brookes wrote:

> The original owner [of Cliff House], long dead, was known to be very attached to the place: I am willing to believe he returned to see how we were treating his earthly home, and finding it rejuvenated and filled with young people and activity, went satisfied on his way.
>
> For many years now [1956] we have not heard of him ... [p.275]

Perhaps the occurrence of another 'ghostly visitor' – this time, one she knew well – had convinced her.

Mabel's mother died in 1943 and bequeathed the contents of *Raveloe* (Mabel's childhood home) to her granddaughter. Much of her vast collection of art, mahogany furniture and Oriental antiques were subsequently dispersed at public auction, and two of the three auctions were held on-site at *Raveloe*.

Mabel wrote that she felt her mother's presence at these auctions.

> Later, when the Air Force took over Raveloe and the furnishings were replaced by desks, chairs and filing cabinets, mother appeared one evening.
>
> Two security police-officers on duty, locking up after the departure of the clerks, saw to their astonishment an old lady, white-haired, small in build, leave the sitting-room and mount the stairs, gathering up her long black skirt as she went, and disappear round the bend to the landing.
>
> They thought for a moment she might be a cleaner staying late at work, and started after her, calling out that nobody was allowed in the building after hours.
>
> A day or two later, at about the same time, she walked towards

them in the ballroom. One startled man cried, 'My God, <u>you</u> here again,' and she turned, gave him a glance of admonition, and went past towards the stairs.

They reported the happening to headquarters as beyond the scope of security. Later they saw her again in the billiard-room and then no more: nor has she been seen again ... [Dame Mabel Brookes, Crowded Galleries, London, 1956, p. 279]

Mabel Brookes was made a CBE in 1933, a Dame of the British Empire in 1955, and was awarded an honorary LLD by Monash University in 1967.

She died on 30th April 1975, and to date, has not been reported as taking up residence in either *Raveloe* or *Cliff House*.

☼

[Privately owned]

11. The Convict's Revenge

'the ghostly figure desperately kept his grip...'

The Moreton Bay Penal Settlement, founded on the banks of the Brisbane River in 1824, gave rise to two interlocked ghost accounts within six years – a paradoxical battle between 'freedom' and 'tyranny'.

This was no ordinary penal settlement:

> It was a special hell established for the purpose of disciplining those who had offended the penal system in the older colony of the south. The men and women sent there had all been convicted of new offences since their arrival in Australia. The rate of survival [at Moreton Bay] was not high ... [Sunday Mail (Brisbane), 12 January 1941, p.2]

The camp Commandant from 1825 to 1830, Captain Patrick Logan, was no ordinary man, either.

> Overbearing in his manner towards the prisoners, and always willing to meet the exigencies of a small offence by ordering punishment at the triangle [i.e. lashes], it is not a matter of wonder that his reign was spoken of as one of terror.
>
> It was not necessary to commit a heinous offence to merit the displeasure and prescribed punishment of the Commandant; the faintest murmur against a task allotted or inability to perform the work was sufficient to secure for the unfortunate delinquent from 50 to 100 lashes, and these were not laid on with a light hand. [www.brisbanehistory.com/convict_era.html]

Moreton Bay, Queensland

Convicts who escaped from Moreton Bay into the surrounding bush land were deemed to be 'highwaymen' if not rounded up and caught within 24 hours. The penalty for 'highwaymen' was 300 lashes. Logan sometimes increased this to 500.

For some hapless convicts, this was their final punishment before they 'gave up the ghost'.

Indeed, some convicts preferred death in the bush to Logan's severe penalties and, when escapees were surrounded by troops, often provoked their captors to achieve that end.

> The Moreton Bay Free Press, an early Brisbane newspaper, featured an account of how a convict known as Stimson was one of the convicts to find the cruel treatment under Captain Logan more than he could bear.
>
> He escaped to the bush not once but three times, with the severity of hundreds of lashes declared as the proper punishment. This he endured for his first and second attempts, forcing him to use shrewd methods to resist recapture the third time. [Valerie and Timothy McKenzie, A Glimpse of Ghosts, Sydney, 1984, p 105]

Alas, Stimson had little chance of hiding from his captors. Captain Logan knew all the country in the south-western ranges of the Brisbane River watershed. During his time at Moreton Bay, he had undertaken many exploratory trips into the wild terrain inland of Moreton Bay, often alone, surveying and mapping the district.

> [Stimson's] tricks were hopelessly foiled, and he was hunted until he was totally exhausted and starving in the hot, dry bush. He was shown no mercy and was sentenced to death at the triangle. [Valerie and Timothy McKenzie, A Glimpse of Ghosts, Sydney, 1984, p 105]

Yes, Logan's sentence was that Stimson be flogged until he died!

At dusk one day while returning home on horseback alone from one of his forays into the bush, Captain Logan saw a man standing beside the track watching him. As the man was dressed in familiar yellow convict garb, Logan knew instantly he'd found an absconder and commanded him to walk ahead of his horse back to the settlement.

Instead, to Logan's surprise, the convict advanced towards Logan and grabbed his stirrup. Angered by such insolence, Logan raised his riding crop and struck down hard on the convict's head – but the whip seemed to pass right through the man and instead landed a sharp blow to his horse's flank!

> The horse reacted with wild bucking, but the ghostly figure desperately kept his grip on the stirrup.
>
> Despite this the Commandant struck out viciously time and time again at his attacker, without any success...the horse bolted ... as suddenly as a gust of wind, the eerie convict-garbed figure disappeared into the shadows.
>
> Patrick Logan ... had seen the ghost of Stimson, the convict whom he ordered to be flogged and who had been dead only one month to the day, at precisely the spot where Stimson had been captured for the third and last time. [Valerie and Timothy McKenzie, A Glimpse of Ghosts, Sydney, 1984, p. 106]

In early October, 1830, knowing he was shortly to be posted back to Sydney, Captain Logan set off on his final mapping survey. There was a small creek west of the Limestone Hills outpost (Ipswich) he needed to track in order to complete his map of the area for the benefit of his successor.

Together with his batman and five trusted convicts, he set off towards Mount Irwin. For most of this journey, the party was stalked by hostile aborigines who twice attacked the group and were driven off.

A week later, the mapping task completed and Logan's notes written up, the party set off to return to the settlement. Inexplicably, on October 17, the Captain decided to send his men ahead while he went off exploring further, arranging a rendezvous and time to catch up later in the day.

> When he found he could not reach the spot before nightfall, Logan built a rough shelter and settled down for the night. [University of Queensland, espace.library]

His men waited at the meeting point all that day and the next, but Logan did not arrive.

Moreton Bay, Queensland

Around midday the following day, a group of convicts working on the Brisbane River bank saw Logan on horseback on the opposite side of the river. He was waving to attract their attention. Two prisoners immediately dropped their tools, ran to the punt and rowed across the river to pick up Captain Logan, as was their usual custom.

When they arrived, there was no sign of man nor beast. Hardly surprising, considering Captain Logan had been brutally murdered the previous night!

Ten days later, searchers found the temporary shelter where Logan had slept, fully clothed, on the night of October 17. It was evident he had been attacked while sleeping. He had managed to escape to his horse—which he mounted without bridle or saddle—and rode off into the night.

By carefully following the tracks of the horse, they found Logan's lifeless body buried face down in a shallow grave – horribly mutilated and disfigured. Nearby his scattered notes were found, torn and shredded, along with several items of clothing, including his boots.

Who murdered and mutilated the sadistic Captain Logan? Certainly, there were many who desired nothing more than to seek revenge on the bloodthirsty Commandant.

> Some maintain that the murder was not perpetrated by blacks, or if it was, the deed was done at the instigation of revengeful convicts who had succeeded in escaping from his terrible rule.
> [www.brisbanehistory.com/convict_era.html]

However, it is intriguing to note that the spot on which the ghost of Logan was clearly observed by the convicts across the river was precisely where convict Stimson had been captured for the third time before being flogged to death, and where his ghost returned to grapple with Logan, attempting to pull him from his mount before disappearing into the shadows.

Just an eerie coincidence? Or could it be that Captain Logan and convict Stimson are destined to continue their endless struggle in an other-worldly realm?

12. A Piteous Moan ... No Bull!

'it was as if the huge animal had never existed'.

We all hope that when we die, those who loved us will miss us and grieve for us. But what becomes of a man whose work requires him to spend most of his time in isolation, far from civilization? Would anyone even notice he was missing, let alone dead? Who would grieve for a man few people even knew?

But wait, I'm getting ahead of myself! Allow me to set the scene as it occurred in the 1870s.

When a group of gentlemen friends spent a pleasant weekend fishing and shooting together on the Murrumbidgee River, not far from Murrumbateman, one of the party suddenly came running back to camp. Breathless and frightened, he announced that he had been chased by a mad bull half a mile down the flat.

One of the group—William Davis, Jnr.—was also the owner of the property on which they were gathered.

> Mr. Davis, taking up his rifle, and observing, 'That brute is not fit to be let live,' asked some of the party to accompany him to the shooting of it. [Queanbeyan Age, 19 July 1910, p. 2]

Known locally as the 'Squire of Ginninderra', Davis' skill

Yass, N.S.W.

with the rifle was well known. The following incident was even mentioned in his obituary in 1910:

> Four of them went; but there was only one rifle. In due time the enraged beast was sighted, and first pawing the ground he came on to charge the party. 'Don't one of you move; keep shoulder to shoulder close to me,' said the man with the rifle [Davis]. On came the beast; and when within less than ten yards of the party, and with a bullet in his forehead, it fell dead almost at their feet.
> [Queanbeyan Age, 19 July 1910, p. 2]

Later, William's brother Alfred was riding his horse not far away on their property beside the Murrumbidgee River near the Limestone Plains.

> I was fifty yards from the gunyah* at the Washpen where I saw the dead body of a man; I went to my brother and returned with him, and rode up to within three yards of the body; I could not tell then whose body it was; the skull was broken; I informed the police.
> [Alfred Davis in Canberra Cavalcade: Tales of the People and Legends of Southern N.S.W., Robert Wilson, Canberra, 1996, p. 98] *Gunyah: a simple bark shelter framed with tree branches – often built by shepherds, copying Aboriginal examples.

Senior Sergeant Martin Brennan of Queanbeyan police, took the coroner, Dr Blake, a local doctor, Dr Perry, and a constable to The Washpen and located the victim.

> The body was found lying in the same condition as [previously] discovered. The top of the head was entirely gone, and the face eaten away apparently by native cats. The separation of the upper portion of the skull had the appearance of being effected by some sharp instrument, so clean were the edges of the remaining portion, and the brains are supposed to have been 'scooped' out, in there were no torn membranes left to lead to the supposition that they had been devoured or picked by native cats. ... [Cornwall Chronicle quoting Yass Courier, 19 July 1876, p.4]

Was this a prior victim of the 'mad bull'? Not unless the bull carried a gun!

> The medical gentleman's evidence states that the deceased's death resulted from a gunshot wound, and what appeared to be a small piece of metal, which looked like lead, was extracted from the remaining portion of the skull... [Cornwall Chronicle quoting Yass Courier, 19 July 1876, p.4]

The mutilated victim was identified as Jeremiah McCarthy, a shepherd employed by Davis, whose work at that time required him to spend long periods in isolation.

> In New South Wales the year 1876 was a terrible one. Drought ruled the land, The triangle of country enclosed by Queanbeyan, Goulburn, and Yass had no real rain for months. To keep stock alive it was necessary to keep them moving from one starved pasture to another... the homestead was miles distant. The curlew, the goanna, the crow, and the dingo constituted the [shepherd's] only company. [The World's News, Sydney, 27 July 1937, p. 10]

The body was hastily buried, wrapped in two of his own blankets, beside his rough gunyah close to the Murrumbidgee River.

> The murdered man appears to have been above the ordinary run of men of his class, as shown by his studious habits, his possession of a book of classical and other high literature ... It is not easy to account for the murderer's object – whether it was revenge for a wrong, the issue of a quarrel, or a desire to possess himself of the goods of his victim. [Queanbeyan Age, 20 July 1876, p. 2]

It would be easy to assume that such a cultured man – one who was so gruesomely murdered and left to rot miles from civilization—might become a restless soul condemned to roam the Murrumbidgee River until his murderer was found and brought to justice.

This was not so, but there may have been another who remained after death to show remorse for such a gentle soul.

Police from Yass and Queanbeyan worked together to unravel the mystery. They discovered a set of strange footprints in a nearby creek bed – both made by left foot boots, one larger than the other and worn by a singular person!

They tracked the footprints, strange as they were, several miles towards the residence of William Davis, the 'Squire of Ginninderra.' Davis told them he suspected the notorious Tom Robinson, also known as 'Waterloo Tom', a ruffian who he had recently found in his kitchen at a late hour. He explained:

Yass, N.S.W.

> ...he had in his possession a rife-bore gun, the barrel of which was nearly six feet long, and which he called 'Long Tom' ... On the following morning he could find no trace of the fiend, who had cleared out during the early hours, taking with him a blanket, a left foot boot, and a canister of strychnine. [Martin Brennan, Reminiscences of the Goldfields and Elsewhere, Sydney, 1907, pps. 312-313]

On the fifth day of their search, Senior Sergeant Brennan and Constable McIntosh caught up with Robinson near the slopes of Black Mountain, and despite his protestations of innocence, took him into custody.

> Brennan described Waterloo Tom as being a man of colossal height and heavily bearded. He was missing the sight of one eye and limped with an injured knee. He carried his rifle everywhere and in his belt a vicious knife made from the sharpened point of a scythe. [Canberra Cavalcade, Robert Wilson, Canberra, 1996, p. 99]

He was even wearing two left boots!

In preparing the prosecution case, it became necessary to exhume McCarthy's body. They arrived at the site around 2 o'clock. Martin Brennan describes what happened next:

> We commenced the work of exhumation, and just as the spade had touched a timber slab which rested on the body, the sound of a terrific explosion took place, the ground trembled and seemed to sink beneath our feet, as if from the impact of a monster thunderbolt, or aerolite hurled by Jupiter, father of gods and men, against our planet, and a rumbling sound of great volume reverberated through the valley for some seconds.
>
> Before we had recovered ourselves however from this appalling experience, a roar was heard on the mountain top above us, which was intensified by repetitions along the valley of the great river, when suddenly we observed through the gloom a huge bull of immaculate whiteness rushing down the declivity towards us.
> [Martin Brennan, Reminiscences of the Goldfields and Elsewhere, Sydney, 1907, p. 317]

What? An earth tremor, followed by a bellowing white bull charging them! Don't mess with dead fellows!

Martin Brennan continues:

> We promptly sought the protection of trees close by, drew

revolvers, and stood in readiness for defense, but this was unnecessary, as the animal, on reaching the open grave, stopped suddenly, and with head erect, surveyed the surroundings, pawed the earth for a few seconds, then lay down beside the grave, moaned piteously, and expired.

Martin Brennan, later Police Superintendent, was unable to explain the phenomena he witnessed. 'I merely describe what four police officers, in perfect health, and with all their faculties unimpaired, saw and carefully observed in the day time, and which, after many years' service in the police force, they are unable to account for,' he said.

The tale of the roaring white bull spread rapidly on the 'bush telegraph' throughout the district. No one had seen such a fine animal around. Who owned it? It was hard to believe that a wild bull could maintain such condition running free in the mountains during a drought without ever being seen by a local. Most were convinced it was no man's property.

But the tale isn't over yet.

Trooper McIntosh from Queanbeyan was sent back to take an inventory of Jeremiah McCarthy's effects. On his way, he was joined by William Davis, the sharp-shooting 'Squire of Ginninderra.', who said he had he had a special interest in the white bull and wanted to look at the carcass.

A special interest? Why? Could Davis have suspected the bull was the one he shot years before?

> When the two men arrived at the shepherd's hut everything was just as the police had left it two days earlier, except for one thing – the bull had vanished!
>
> There were no marks where it had fallen beside the grave, no tracks to suggest it had been moved and no trace of blood, bone or hide to indicate that it had been butchered on the spot or eaten by dingoes or goannas.
>
> In fact, as the trooper remarked to Davis, it was as if the huge animal had never existed. [Richard Davis, Great Australian Ghost Stories, Sydney, 2012, p.106]

Was Davis right? Is it possible that gentle Jeremiah McCarthy—living and working as he did in isolation for months at a time—had formed a special friendship with the angry beast when both were still alive?

Had the bull been attempting to protect Jeremiah when the shooters arrived in the area?

Perhaps Jeremiah's gruesome murder enraged 'the mad bullock' one more time after his death, prompting him to return and demonstrate his sorrow ...

> ... on reaching the open grave [the animal] ... lay down beside the grave, moaned piteously, and expired.

Tom Robinson was found guilty of the murder of the cultured shepherd, Jeremiah McCarthy, and was sentenced to life imprisonment.

The raging bull was never seen again.

13. Old Henry's Ghost

'Old Henry's' hobnailed boots have been heard climbing the lighthouse's spiral staircase'

In 2001 a family group gathered at Point Hicks Lighthouse on the eastern shores of Victoria for a special birthday celebration. They signed the 'Visitor's Book' to record the occasion, and wrote 'Happy Birthday' in the comments column. Then they were joined by the lightkeepers, Rob and Amanda Coates, in lighting a hundred candles to sing the traditional 'Happy Birthday to You'.

'Old Henry,' alias Robert Grace Christorfen, was 100 years old, but he only lived for 46 years. For the past 54 years had been Point Hicks' resident ghost.

> We exchanged notes and photographs, and although the ghost did not appear to help us blow the candles out, we hope he knew there were three generations [of his descendants] there to wish him well.
> [Margaret Christopher & Robert Haldine, Lighthouses of Australia Monthly Bulletin, April 2001]

The family of Robert Grace Christorfen proudly acknowledged their family heritage.

Born in 1901 at Dandenong, he joined the Victoria Police as a 23-year-old, and nine years later, after serving as a mounted trooper and as a foot constable, he was asked to resign because – horror of horrors—he was allegedly living with a woman who was not his wife!

After struggling through the Depression years, he enlisted as a private in the 16th Australian Infantry Training Battalion in 1940 and shipped off to Palestine five months later. Shortly afterwards he was reported 'missing in action' in Crete.

He had been captured by German troops, along with many other Australian soldiers, and interned in the infamous Stalag XIII-C in Bavaria, Germany. He was officially registered as a German prisoner-of-war in October 1941 and remained there for the duration of WWII.

Following his Army discharge in September 1945, all Christorfen wanted was 'peace and quiet' in his homeland countryside. And he got it ... for a rather short period.

He became an Assistant Lighthouse-keeper at Point Hicks lighthouse in Victoria. His wife Daisy accompanied him, and they lived in one of two keeper's cottages next to the light.

Point Hicks, like Robert Grace Christorfen himself, has an interesting background.

> There is a simple white monument on the headland with a plaque that reads: 'Lieutenant James Cook R,N. of the Endeavour first sighted Australia near this point which he named Point Hicks after Lieutenant Zachary Hicks who first saw the land. April 19th (Ship's Log Date) April 20th (Calendar Date) 1770.'
> [www.aussietowns.com.au]

The lighthouse, built in 1887-88, stands 130ft / 40m high—the tallest mass concrete lighthouse in Australia—and was first lit in May 1890.

With its comparative isolation, Robert Christorfen enjoyed his new freedom at Point Hicks despite the strict regularity his work demanded. But the pleasures were relatively short-lived.

His daughter-in-law, Margaret Christopher [married to his son, also named Robert], explained over fifty years later:

> On the 3 April 1947 he went to check the cray pots on the rocks near the keeper's cottage. According to news clippings and folk

lore, Daisy went to call him for breakfast. He said he would be in soon, but was never seen again.

A search was organized but was unsuccessful. He was a strong swimmer but perhaps he was knocked unconscious by the fall.
[Margaret Christopher, Lighthouses of Australia Monthly Bulletin, April 2001]

There is some doubt about the cause of Christorfen's death because his body was never found. A year before the family gathering for the Light-keeper's 100th birthday, Lighthouses of Australia *Bulletin* published a letter (February, 2000) from a different relative revealing 'sources in the family suggested foul play was involved.'

The writer said his deceased grandmother (name supplied) said Light-keeper Robert Christorfen was her brother. Their father was Gustav Christorfen, a Norwegian ships-carpenter who 'jumped ship' in Melbourne. The writer also stated ' My grandmother was quite certain that 'She did him in' – inferring that Daisy had committed homicide.

There had been a heavy sea running the morning Christorfen disappeared and an accidental slip as suggested by his daughter-in-law could logically explain it. The police searched up and down the coast for six days without result.

With or without help, the Point Hicks Assistant Lightkeeper had presumably drowned – but his spirit remains.

Subsequent light-keepers and visitors tell of seeing or hearing his apparition moving around the station. Shirley & Stuart Buchanan, inveterate light-keepers and lighthouse devotees, spent their seven-months leave visiting lighthouses around Australia and learnt directly from the Point Hicks head light-keeper, Ray Wilde and his wife Edna, about the Point Hicks ghost:

Many light-keepers over the years had sighted the ghost near the lighthouse. In the 1950s, when the light was still kerosene powered, a light-keeper who spent his nightly watches playing the violin in the lighthouse, swore that he saw the ghost on numerous occasions. [Stuart Buchanan, The Lighthouse Keepers, Sanford, Qld., 1994, p. 154]

More recently, when Jim McMinn, Head-Keeper at Point Hicks took his long service leave Ray & Kaye Kirkwood, relieving keepers, spent eight months at Point Hicks working with acting Head-Keepers, Alan & Marilyn Staag.

Ray wrote about his experiences on various Australian light-stations in his book *Variant Breed: Confessions of a Light-Keeper*. Here's his comments on 'Old Henry':

> 'Old Henry' was the affectionate name presented to the Point Hicks ghost, believed to be an expired light-keeper, Christorfen, who drowned after falling off rocks below the tower.
>
> Alan and Marilyn had warned us of 'Old Henry' who roamed freely throughout the whole station; into the houses of keepers; inside the beacon; everywhere, we had also been warned previously by many others as well, even before we arrived here, about the antics of our 'Old Henry.'
>
> His body was never recovered; years later a skull was found off the coast of New Zealand believed to have belonged to that particular gentleman.
>
> 'Old Henry', literally, had been seen thousands of times by many light-keepers serving on the station, and by hundreds of visitors alike, with their descriptions documented...
>
> During the eight months or so spent at Point Hicks 'Old Henry' never made his presence felt to any of us, including Alan and Marilyn Staag, although both of them had experiences with him on many occasions before. [Ray Kirkwood, Variant Breed: Confessions of a Light-Keeper, Wordclay, 2010]

'Old Henry's' hobnailed boots have been heard climbing the 162 steps of the lighthouse's spiral staircase, and in the pantry of the keeper's cottage where – over 70 years earlier – he'd lived with Daisy. He has been known to polish the brass doorknobs, open air vents, and move tools around.'

As Ray Kirkwood wrote in his book:

'Old Henry never hurt anyone.'

His spirit simply didn't wish to leave the place where he had felt contentment for once during his short 46 years of earthly life.

☼

14. A Chinese Gift for Lovers

'it continued urging haste with skeletal fingers.'

During the 1870's Australian gold rush, people from all over the county – and indeed, from other parts of the world—flocked to the rivers and streams of the remote bush searching for those elusive nuggets. Fortunes were made and lost in a few short years, but at least one who struck it lucky did not live long enough to enjoy his riches.

Perhaps, though, he spent more than half a century guarding it.

The Palmer River in Northern Queensland, site of the richest alluvial goldfields in Australia, flows west from the Great Dividing Range, and joins the Mitchell River which empties into the Gulf of Carpentaria in the far north of Australia.

Gold was first found in the sandy river bed in 1872 and by the following year over 30,000 people were spread along the river and its tributaries. Mass migration of oriental miners from southern China outnumbered the European population, causing considerable resentment.

When the gold ran out, the settlements were abandoned. One of these – the thriving settlement of Limestone—once had six hotels and several stores, but it, too, fell into disrepair by the early part of the 20th century.

Nature claimed its small cemetery, its gravestones were flattened, and the old Chinese joss house with its tiled roof and scattered porcelain ornaments soon became a crumbling ruin.

In 1941, a young couple wandered into the deserted old settlement of Limestone...

> ... a nineteen-year-old boy with a Chinese father and an Australian mother who, it is alleged, had abducted a sixteen-year-old girl, the child of an Aboriginal mother and a Spanish father. [Frank Cusack (ed.), Australian Ghost Stories, Melbourne, 1967, p. 45]

Abducted? Not so! This young couple from Cooktown only had eyes for each other, but their parents had forbidden them to marry.

> The Spanish father swore he would strangle his daughter rather than see her marry a 'heathen Chinaman' and the Anglo-Saxon mother threatened to disown her son if he married a 'papist black gin'. Tempers flared, nerves frayed, unretractable words were spoken and arguments raged in both families through the long tropic nights. [Richard Davis, Great Australian Ghost Stories, Sydney, 2012, pps. 125-126]

The besotted teenagers refused to be parted. They fled into the bush, with only a vague plan to hide out and be together. Alas, their absence was reported to the police and a search party was sent out to round them up. They were located just two weeks later.

> The girl had wept bitterly when she learned that the boy, who, for convenience, is called Tommy Foo, was to be charged with abducting her and would probably be sent to gaol. [Sunday Mail, 9 February 1941, p.4]

Hearing of the charge, a group of Cooktown people, lead by the local doctor, testified to Tommy Foo's character and previous good behavior, and sought to have the charge set aside.

When the police discovered that Tommy was more than willing to marry his beloved Mary, they relented, but they still had one reservation. When Tommy was searched, the police had found a quantity of gold in small nuggets and a number of sovereigns in his possession – together worth

Palmer River, Queensland

several hundreds of pounds. In those days, that was a small fortune!

It was known that neither of the runaways had any money when they left Cooktown weeks earlier. How had Tommy obtained such a large amount?

Although he realized he might be charged with theft if he failed to provide the police with a satisfactory response, he kept silent.

> Where then had Tommy got the gold and sovereigns when wandering through the bush? He might have located the gold itself in some uncombed corner of a diggings, but not even the luck of a Chinaman – and Tommy was half Chinaman – would account for a penniless lad finding sovereigns in the jungles of Cape York Peninsula. [Sunday Mail, 9 February 1941, p.4]

The police confiscated Tommy's 'loot,' confident the real owner would soon report its loss and make a claim for its return.

Grateful for the community support they received, the love-struck teens discussed whether they should tell the police how they came by such a windfall. But who would believe their story? Mary was worried that if they told the truth and weren't believed, Tommy would probably be charged with theft.

Eventually, the couple agreed to confess. Perhaps the truth would set them free to marry.

Tommy explained that he and his girlfriend had wandered through the bush, staying away from the main tracks to avoid travelers, and living off the land by catching game and fish.

> One afternoon when they came down a rough, winding mountain track and saw below them the remains of a township, they stood for a long time, surveying it before going closer. It was only after exercising the closest observation for some hours that they decided the township was deserted, without a single inhabitant.
>
> Curiously they explored the tumble-down buildings, the overgrown streets, and the unkempt cemetery. [Sunday Mail, 9 February 1941, p.4]

GHOSTS DOWN UNDER

They slept that night on the broken floor of an old hut.

Some time in the night the lad woke and was startled to see the outline of a figure in the open doorway. He first thought was that it was a policeman or a tracker. But he remained silent and did not move.

The figure seemed to glow suddenly brighter and he could perceive that the face was that of a Chinese. It raised its arm in a beckoning movement that was repeated three times. The lad froze. A moment later the apparition had disappeared. [Frank Cusack, Australian Ghost Stories, Melbourne, 1967, p.46]

Tommy shook Mary awake and told her what he'd seen. She dismissed it as a dream and immediately went back to sleep. Tommy stayed alert, keeping his eyes on the doorway, frightened the vision might return. Although he was fearful, he recognized that his duty was to protect Mary. He determined they would leave at daybreak.

Luck deserted them. At dawn, just as they were ready to leave, they heard the sound of horses approaching. A group of noisy gold prospectors rode into Limestone to rest their horses. Tommy and Mary stayed hidden, keeping a watchful eye on the intruders from a safe distance.

The rough prospectors remained until late afternoon. By the time they remounted and rode away it was growing dark, so the star-crossed lovers reluctantly agreed to stay another night in their hide-away. At least it provided some protection against the elements.

All was quiet until just before midnight. Something startled Tommy and Mary into full wakefulness.

The oriental specter again stood in the open doorway!

They both saw its hollow face. They both felt the urgency of its beckoning gestures. They got to their feet and were compelled to follow as it continued urging haste with skeletal fingers.

Along the rough, weed grown street he led, always beckoning. As if hitched to him, Tommy and Mary followed. Right to the wall of the temple the specter went, making no sound. It stopped beside the urn and bending, touched it, pointing back at Tommy, and again at the urn.

Palmer River, Queensland

Then like a whiff of smoke the specter was gone. And they were alone. With one accord the pair fled to their ruined hut and trembled there until dawn. [Sunday Mail, 9 February 1941, p.4]

Before leaving Limestone (or what was left of it) at daybreak, their curiosity was piqued by the joss-house urn. They decided to re-examine it in daylight.

Everything seemed as it had been when the specter led them to the site the previous night. Tommy pulled the urn's stopper out and tilted it over.

Clearly scratched on the bottom of the urn, in Chinese characters that Tommy could read, was the name Feng Ching Loo. His fine ashes scattered into a loose pile on the ground.

Tommy had hopes it might contain something of value, but seeing only ashes around his feet, he threw the urn roughly on the ground and it broke apart.

> It split from top to bottom, and there rolled from the lower end a small heap of nuggets and a score of sovereigns.
>
> While Mary gathered up this sudden wealth, Tommy examined the broken urn. A false bottom had been constructed in it by using a shelf of clay within the porcelain, after the gold had been placed within. [Sunday Mail, 9 February 1941, p.9]

They looked at each other in amazement, smiled, and hand-in-hand they left Limestone forever. Just two days later the searching police patrol caught up with them, and they were taken to Cooktown.

The skeptical policeman listened to Tommy's explanation, then chose to continue waiting for a claimant to come forward. But none did. As impossible as it sounded, the policeman had to wonder whether Tommy's improbable story was true after all.

Eventually, the bullion was handed back to Tommy.

> The story was passed on to the Press of the day and subsequently found its way to China and was repeated in the North China News and other papers there.
>
> As for the ghost of Fen Chen Loo, it was apparently never heard of again. [Frank Cusack, Australian Ghost Stories, Melbourne, 1967, p. 4]

GHOSTS DOWN UNDER

Tommy and Mary married and soon afterwards departed from Cooktown for places unknown. Perhaps they named their first-born Fen Chen Loo in gratitude to the benevolent ghost they encountered in the rugged Australian outback.

15. The Most Celebrated Ghost

*'It let out a long and terrifying moan ...
like the howl of a wounded beast.'*

Australia's most celebrated ghost – that of Frederick Fisher – was not mentioned during his murder trial, but its doubtful the trial would have taken place without his intervention.

Frederick George James Fisher was born in London on 28 August 1792 and made a reasonable living as a shopkeeper, until:

> Fisher obtained possession of forged banknotes, either innocently through his work or deliberately to pass through his shop. He was arrested. tried at the Surrey Gaol Delivery on 26 July 1815 and sentenced to fourteen years' transportation to Australia. [Carol Liston, Campbelltown: The Bicentennial History, Sydney, 1988, p.59]

On arrival, Fisher was sent to Liverpool (40km/25 miles west of Sydney) where, due to his ability to both read and write (unusual qualities for a convict), he was attached to the office of J. T. Campbell, the colonial administrator.

His keen intellect and willingness to work hard stood him in good stead. In 1822, with half his sentence served, Frederick Fisher applied for – and was granted – a ticket-of-leave. This enabled him to move freely around the colony and purchase land.

He wasted no time. By 1825 he owned four small farms all under cultivation and averaging around 40acres/16 hectares each. His prized possession was the property at Campbell Town (57km/35 miles S-W of Sydney)

> He owned a farm of thirty acres which fronted what was then the main street of Campbell Town and is now Queen Street. It adjoined that of another ticket-of-leave men, George Worrall.
> [Frank Cusack ed. Australian Ghost Stories, London, 1967, p.3]

Indeed, Fisher and his neighbor, George Worrall, quickly became 'best mates'.

Not long after, however, a dispute occurred between Fisher and a local carpenter, William Brooker, who confronted Fisher at the Inn demanding payment for work completed. Brooker—who was not exactly sober at the time—became belligerent and aggressive, and Fisher pulled a knife to defend himself.

Although no one was hurt, Fisher knew the score. If Brooker complained to the magistrates, Fisher would serve a gaol term for his actions. Just in case, he gave power of attorney to neighbor and best mate, George Worrall, to enable him to manage his affairs should he be sent to gaol.

Brooker did lodge a complaint, and Fisher did stand trial for his assault. Although he was found guilty, he was given a light sentence and small fine.

That evening, Fisher and Worrall celebrated with three neighbors at one of the town's ramshackle inns. It was the last time anyone saw Frederick Fisher alive!

> The local clergyman, Reverend Thomas Reddall, who doubled as the town's magistrate, was immediately concerned – and questioned Worrall closely. Worrall claimed that [Fisher], fearful of being discovered in a fraudulent property deal, had decamped to Sydney and from there returned by ship to England. [John Pinkney, Haunted, The Book of Australian Ghosts, Melbourne, 2005, p.74]

About three weeks later, George Worrall began selling some of Fisher's belongings, claiming he had bought them from Fisher just prior to his departure.

> Suspicions began to arise, however, when Worrall tried to sell one of Fisher's horses and the prospective buyer demanded proof of

ownership. Worrall produced an obviously forged receipt that he said he had been given when he bought the horse from Fisher.
[Richard Davis, Great Australian Ghost Stories, (Sydney, 2012) p.52]

Worrall boldly approached a local solicitor, James Norton, seeking the title to Fisher's farm. Norton suspected something was astray and refused to furnish the title deeds. Instead, he wrote to the Attorney-General, suggesting there might be a connection between Fisher's disappearance and Worrall's interest in his assets.

A week later, Worrall was arrested on suspicion of Fisher's murder.

The Colonial Secretary's Office placed the following notice in *The Australian* newspaper on September 23, 1826:

SUPPOSED MURDER

WHERAS FREDERICK FISHER BY THE SHIP Atlas, holding a Ticket of Leave, and lately residing at Campbell Town, has disappeared within these last three weeks – it is hereby notified that a reward of twenty pounds will be given for the discovery of the body of the said Frederick Fisher, or if he shall have quitted the Colony, a reward of five pounds will be given to any person or persons who shall produce proof of the same.

Almost a month passed without any news of Frederick Fisher, so the Campbell Town police were instructed to intensify their search for Fisher's body.

Then, two lads named Rixon and Burrows were taking a short-cut home through Fisher's farm when they made a startling discovery. They noticed bloodstains on the post-and-rail boundary fence, which they reported immediately to the local police.

Constable Luland began a second search of the area around Fisher's farm. A lock of hair—the same color as Fisher's—and a tooth were found. Then he searched the marshy paddock, poking an iron bar into the soil, hoping to find a buried body.

Nothing was found.

Then, a local farmer names James Farley decided to take a stroll down Queen Street late one night.

GHOSTS DOWN UNDER

About 400 meters from Fisher's shack, Farley spotted a figure sitting on the top rail of a fence. As he drew closer he realized, to his horror, that it was Frederick Fisher—not the living, breathing man that he had seen and spoken to many times, but Fisher's ghost. The pale 'fuzzy' form was bathed in an eerie white light and there was blood dripping from an open wound to its head.

The ghost looked straight at James Farley, its dead eyes holding the living man's in a hypnotic stare. Next it let out a long and terrifying moan which Farley described as like the howl of a wounded beast. Then it raised its right arm, extending a quivering finger and pointed in the direction of the creek that flowed behind Fisher's farm. [Richard Davis, Great Australian Ghost Stories, Sydney, 2012, p.53]

Farley fainted at the sight of the ghost, and later staggered home and collapsed again at his own front door. He was put to bed in a state of shock, and stayed there for ten days!

When he came back to his senses, Farley notified the local magistrate who ordered a search of the local creek in the direction indicated by the ghost.

Gilbert—an aboriginal tracker from Liverpool – was also called in to assist the searchers. Gilbert tasted the water in several ponds and shook his head. Then, when he tasted water from another large puddle, he announced: 'white fellow's fat there!'

They followed this string of puddles, prodding the damp ground beneath it as they went, and found Fisher's body in a shallow, watery grave on George Worrall's land.

> The body was partially decomposed, a 'saddened death-like sickly white' and the flesh fell from the hands and feet when touched. The face and head had been shockingly disfigured but the clothes, a plum-colored jacket, a full-blown shirt and buckles on the braces were easily recognizable as Fisher's. [Carol Liston, Campbelltown: the Bicentennial History, Sydney, 1988, p.63]

On February 2, 1827, George Worrall appeared before Chief Justice Francis Forbes in the criminal Court of Sydney. As he was the only person who stood to benefit from Fisher's death, the jury found him guilty, He was sentenced to death and executed three days later.

On the scaffold, he confessed to a clergyman that he killed, mutilated and buried Frederick Fisher.

References to ghosts cannot be alluded to in a court of justice, nor can they be introduced as evidence to account for any course of action taken, but James Farley maintained to his deathbed in 1841 that he had seen a ghost. He is widely quoted as saying 'I speak only the truth. I saw that ghost as plainly as I see you now.'

The good people of Campbell Town (now spelt as one word) accepted the 'Ghost on the Fence-rail' account without question. They embraced it, in fact. It has become Campbelltown's most enduring legend. Some would say it is Australia's most celebrated ghost story.

Since 1956, Campbelltown has held an annual 10-day 'Fisher's Ghost Festival' featuring a street parade, an art award, fun run, street fair, craft exhibition and a giant carnival with fireworks. Not bad for an event which happened over century ago!

While outsiders refer to 'Fisher's Ghost', most locals use an abbreviated form of his given name, 'Fred' – and treat him like a familiar. It seems that when things run smoothly at Campbelltown, Fred is quite happy. If he's displeased, or 'simply in a larrikin mood, he makes sure everyone knows about it'!

GHOSTS DOWN UNDER

> It is generally accepted among locals that Fred must be honoured by the annual parades we hold in his name as they are constantly a success ... the late, great Clive Tregear – our mayor during the late 1960's and early 1970's – always paid due homage and told me it was 'not unreasonable' for anyone to believe in the ghost.
>
> The stories of Fred's activity certainly multiply at the southern end of Queen Street, where Fisher once had his farm and where he was murdered.
>
> Most are now convinced he is a friendly ghost, just mischievous, and call out his name when things go wrong. [Jeff McGill, Campbelltown-Macarthur Advertiser, 21 June, 2006, p.2]

As an example of a series of events incurring 'Fisher's disproval' we look back to the 1970's:

> Workmen at Fisher's Ghost Creek dug up an old railing from an early version of the bridge and the promoter of the Campbelltown Picnic Races, Deirdre O'Dowd, had it restored and used as the finishing post at the 1973 event.
>
> As Deirdre said: 'Fred wasn't very impressed. The rain was so heavy, the horses 'swam' up the track so we had to cancel. Rescheduled for a fortnight later, that event too was a washout, as was the next attempt in 1974. More attempts to stage the event were also inundated and a lot of media attention was generated.
>
> It made the front page news when race club secretary Bob McWilliam eventually dug up the old post and ceremoniously handed it back, ordering Deirdre to remove it from the Appin race track [16kms south of Campbelltown].
>
> And yes—the sun shone gloriously and crowds flocked to the next event. [Jeff McGill, Campbelltown-Macarthur Advertiser, 21 June, 2006), p.135]

'Fred' gets blamed for practically everything that goes astray at Campbelltown's Town Hall Theatre, too:

> Theatre group president Mr. Neil Hatchman recalled in 1995, that he was 'working there a lot at night by myself taking rubbish around the back when the lights went off.' Not alarmed as it was an old building, he found a light switch and turned the lights back on, only to see the shadowy figure of a man moving across the stage.

Hatchman called for him to stop, but the figure ignored him and disappeared into a nearby room. Now somewhat worried, Hatchman picked up a lump of wood and entered the room, only to find it empty. [J. G. Montgomery, Haunted Australia: Ghosts of the Great South Land, Pennsylvania, 2016, p.55]

More recently, also in the early 1990s, the then Mayor of Campbelltown, Jim Kremmer, and his deputy John Hennessy, proposed building a statue to commemorate Fisher's Ghost. 'Fred' apparently did not like the idea at all.

Soon afterwards, the project collapsed. Cr. Kremmer lost his mayorship, and Dr. Hennesy was not re-elected.

Make no mistake. Fred Fisher is still a very real inhabitant of Campbelltown!

16. Suffer the Little Children

An unseen force seemed to be lifting the child and trying to drive her head-first into the glass paneled door!

In January 1980, a group of parents and children from the Rockingham Little Athetics Club traveled to York in the Avon valley, about 100kms east of Perth, for a 5-day camping holiday.

They selected a hostel which shared the facilities of the deserted, 84-year-old York Hospital.

The party consisted of twenty-eight children and five supervising adults—including the club coach, 20-year-old Paul Harrison, and his mother, Joan, who organized the camp.

Their journey was made in stifling 37°C (99°F) temperature; the bus broke down and there were other delays. The 100km trip took 5 hours!!

It was an omen of things to follow.

The Old York Hospital is an impressive, large, two-storey, red-brick building. The group's sleeping quarters were in an annex at the rear, added many years earlier as the hospital's maternity wing. Attached to the main building were other facilities available to the visitors – a kitchen, dining room and a small sitting room.

A wooden staircase behind the main hospital building linked to a rear verandah on each floor, and double-doors on the ground floor were the hospital's only rear entrance.

Certain internal doors on the ground floor were padlocked. The entire second floor was 'out of bounds' to everyone. A caretaker and his wife (and two Rhodesian Ridgeback dogs) lived in a cottage at the back of the property.

Mrs Maureen Cramer, with her young son and daughter, happily joined the camping party and Maureen agreed to become the group's cook. On arrival, she was disappointed to find that provisions, including cool drinks for the children, ordered three weeks earlier had not been delivered. Undaunted, she set about collecting stores and began preparing their first meal away.

After the children had eaten and gone to bed in the dormitory, the adults sought respite from the heat by laying on the verandah outside the kitchen.

That's when the initial incident occurred:

Suddenly, without warning, the dogs appeared out of the shadows and made what could only be described as a ferocious attack on the group of adults. In the confusion which followed, the caretaker's wife appeared and called the dogs off. The group were very shaken, but by this time most of the children had been awakened and further sleep seemed impossible. The heat inside the dormitory was stifling. [Miriam Howard-Wright, 'Holiday Nightmare', Artlook Magazine, April 1980 p.46]

Joan Harrison suggested everyone, including the children, might be better off sleeping in the upstairs dormitory of the main hospital building – with windows open on both front and rear they were more likely to catch cool breezes up there, AND be safe from the dogs! Everyone knew the second floor hospital dormitory was 'out of bounds'. Too bad. The children's welfare was more important.

Paul Harrison and Maureen Cramer armed themselves with torches and set off to investigate – they couldn't switch lights on because that would signal their presence in the forbidden area.

The surreptitious pair later described part of their experience with Dr Maurice Marsh in a 1989 TV documentary series, *Haunted*, which devoted a segment to the Old York Hospital:

> We got midway along the dormitory and our torches went out – and we had a howling wind coming down from the chimney...
> [Maureen Cramer in Haunted, TV documentary with Dr Maurice Marsh, 1989]

A howling wind? How was that possible? The night was still, with not even a breeze at ground level.

Paul elaborated:

> We walked past the fireplace in the middle of the room and both our torches went out. At first I thought it was just my torch blowing, and I went back three or four times, and again it went on and off – corresponding with when we were in front of the fireplace and then again when we came past the fireplace. When we went past the fireplace by two or three meters it actually went off and came back on again! [Paul Harrison in Haunted, (TV documentary with Dr Maurice Marsh), 1989]

Paul also mentioned a foul stench coming from a small attic room. 'To me,' he said, 'it smelt like something dead – a dead animal or something.'

The 'howling wind', 'blinking torches' and 'foul smell' made Maureen and Paul apprehensive. They also felt the presence of some unseen entity in the room, and retreated hastily downstairs to the others.

Over a cup of tea, they decided to leave the children asleep where they were for the night. Then the Ridgebacks sauntered out of the night's gloom, looked at the visitors, and wandered away back into the darkness, this time showing no interest.

It was then that the moaning began.

It was soft at first, then increasingly louder. 'It was,' Joan Harrison told the documentary crew, 'definitely the sound of a woman crying, in pain, moaning. It was frightening ... very frightening ...'

> They [the adults] all sat and looked at each other petrified. Then with one bound they were out of the room and across to the children. All appeared to be sleeping peacefully. They all checked around the place as much as possible. The caretaker's cottage was in darkness, finally they decided to retire to bed, each leaving all doors open in their building so that the children were well supervised. [Miriam Howard-Wright, 'Holiday Nightmare', Artlook Magazine, April 1980]

Coach Paul Harrison confided to his mother 'Mum, there's something definitely wrong here.'

Before breakfast next morning, Paul was proven correct. His mother, Joan, takes up the story:

> The first thing that happened that morning [Tuesday] was Maureen and I got up to get the children's breakfasts, and went to the kitchen. We got the milk and I had a crockery jug which I put on a bench. As I walked across to Maureen, out of the corner of my eye, I could see this jug lift up and float across the room... [Joan Harrison in Haunted, TV documentary with Dr Maurice Marsh, 1989]

It dropped to the floor and smashed into pieces!

Joan continues:

> It was very hard to believe, and I thought 'Well, that didn't just fall on the floor, it was dropped'. I was shocked – Maureen and I were both shocked!

> Then, the next thing, the stove would turn on and off while you were using it – it would just turn itself on and off! They were very

queer things that happened in that kitchen ... and the doorknob – you'd be standing outside and the door-knob would be spinning, absolutely spinning! There was nobody else on the other side, because we all checked, just spinning by itself! [Joan Harrison in Haunted, TV documentary with Dr Maurice Marsh) 1989]

Further 'very queer things' followed shortly afterwards.

Nine-year-old Kirsty, whose mother was one of the camp supervisors, was in the passageway outside the dining room playing with another little girl. One end of this passage had a door with a glass-panel of unusual thickness, about 3½ to 4 feet [106-122cms] above the floor.

Suddenly Kirsty screamed 'Hold me, hold me! Can't sit down! Stop them, Stop them!' Her playmate grabbed Kirsty's clothing but couldn't steady her. An unseen force seemed to be lifting the child and trying to drive her head-first into the glass paneled door! Fortunately Kirsty had automatically raised her arm to protect her head.

> The whole impact appeared to have been broken with Kirsty's hand, rather than her head, smashing through the glass panel. Joan later said that it was the most uncanny and frightening thing. The child's wrist was in a terrible mess. All the flesh was peeled back almost to the bone to several inches. Yet there was no blood spilled. [Miriam Howard-Wright, EYEWITNESS Australian Ghosts, Artlook Publishers, Perth, 1980 p. 121]

The height of the thick glass made it almost impossible for a small child to fall through the glass. Paul Harrison added, 'The girl was actually thrown through the window, arm first. She had twelve or thirteen stitches inserted in her arm.'

The caretaker was called and took Kirsty and her mother to the local doctor's surgery.

After he returned, Joan Harrison asked him directly about the hysterical moaning heard the previous evening. He jovially told her they had 'heard the Matron.' He told her a local tale that a previous Hospital Matron had been raped, and that she could sometimes be heard running around trying to find her assailant.

Judging by the smirk on his face, Joan felt the caretaker

was making the story up.

> Determined to get to the bottom of the mystery, Joan demanded that he appear that evening at nine o'clock, after the children were asleep, bringing one of his dogs so he could escort the adults, including Joan, to the upstairs part of the building, He arrived at the appointed time, complete with one dog. [Miriam Howard-Wright, 'Holiday Nightmare', Artlook Magazine, April 1980]

The 'inspection party' consisted of the caretaker, Paul the coach, Joan the organizer, Maureen the cook, Mrs Otto and two other mothers who preferred to be unnamed.

Joan and Mrs Otto (and the dog) only got as far as the landing on the stairway between two floors of the hospital. Joan had a serious attack of the 'frights', standing frozen on the landing, seemingly powerless to proceed further up the steps. Similarly, Mrs Otto was too apprehensive to take another step. The dog's hackles were up and it refused to proceed voluntarily – its owner dragged the frightened creature up the stairs by the chain around its neck.

Paul and the three women nervously entered to top floor ward. Eventually overcoming their reticence, those on the stair landing joined them. The caretaker was asked to unlock the small attic room, and Paul and Maureen entered it with him. The dog didn't go inside, but lingered, ready to make a quick exit, with Joan.

The sickly smell was almost overpowering. Paul admitted later he had a choice – hold his breath for long periods or be violently ill. The longer they stayed there, the worse the stench became. All the women promptly returned downstairs, clutching handkerchiefs to their faces.

> Legend has that in the old days patients who had died, and those who were about to die, were kept together in that section of the hospital. Locals call it the Morgue or Dying Room. [Dr Maurice Marsh, Haunted TV documentary, 1989]

Later that night, a bed-check of the children found an 11-year-old boy sitting in his bed, frightened stiff. He was pale and speechless, and clutching his bed-sheets to his chest.

It took quite a while to coax an explanation from him: he

eventually revealed he'd seen a partial human figure materialize beside the door – a face in profile, a shoulder and arm, and a hand resting on the door knob. The rest of this person was, apparently, dematerialized. Paul stayed with the lad until he fell asleep.

The adults, too, had difficulty getting to sleep that night. Apart from the warm, still air making them restless, the moaning and wailing sounds had returned. The 'Matron' was obviously restless as well.

After breakfast the next morning, with rostered chores completed, the group decided to go swimming. Joan and her daughter Charleen, and two other young girls opted to stay behind. They were sitting together in the lounge when the 'Matron's' moaning started again.

Joan was determined not to allow the youngsters to become frightened by the experience, so she did her best to talk over the wailing pretending she couldn't hear it. Certainly, she didn't want them to realize she was afraid. The moaning made no sense to her, and while she considered there was a probably a logical explanation for it, she was in no condition to investigate further.

She took the girls into the kitchen and they helped prepare the lunch. That task completed, she sent them into the garden to play. The noises had ceased by the time the swimming party returned for lunch.

After lunch Maureen Cramer was approached by a distressed young girl who told her there was blood under the stairs, several other children had also seen it.

Paul joined the women and together they tried to fathom this strange phenomenon. It was fresh blood, which seemed to ooze from underneath the staircase. There was no sign of tampering, or of the blood being painted or smeared on the timber surface. Maureen checked the top of the stair, and the higher stairs above the seepage, trying to establish where the blood came from. Without success.

One girl even tasted it; and immediately confirmed it was blood.

Maureen busied herself wiping the blood away and

cleaning the surrounding surfaces. She also had no doubt that it was blood.

A couple of 'minor' incidents played out during the following afternoon, ensuring that the adults, at least, were feeling edgy and 'spooked'.

Joan Harrison felt a sharp shove in the back (by an unseen force), almost strong enough to unseat her from the chair she was sitting on; Maureen Cramer yelled that someone or something had stuck a needle into her head; and coach Paul had a door forcefully slammed in his face (literally) by the same or another unseen force, which then politely opened the door as if to bid him to pass through the doorway.

Paul quickly developed a lump on his cranium to substantiate the incident.

That evening, after the children were settled comfortably in their beds and the adults were together in the sitting room, the moaning and wailing returned.

The adults decided to drag their mattresses to the children's annex and positioned them on the floor close to its two doors. It was an automatic response: the sleeping children in their care had to be protected from any danger, genuine or perceived. They resolved to stay awake all night and, in case slumber overtook them, mops and brooms were placed across the doorways to form a barrier against unwanted intruders. The doors had to remain open because of the unrelenting heat.

It was a bleary-eyed group who greeted the dawning of the next day.

After breakfast, Joan Harrison approached the caretaker again about the 'moaning and crying' and other strange happenings they'd experienced or witnessed. He told her to see her doctor when she went home, laughed, and walked away.

Joan's next surprise was a pleasant one!

She had lost contact with old friends Sylvia and Don who had been in York with their seven children for a few years.

Joan was delightfully surprised when Sylvia called at the camp that afternoon to renew their acquaintance.

They then told Sylvia what they had seen, heard and felt during the previous four days. Sylvia was alarmed and concerned for their well-being and asked if it would be acceptable if she returned with Don, her husband, in the early evening. Everyone agreed.

Around 10.00pm, Don and Paul conducted a thorough torchlight reconnoiter of the grounds and saw nothing unusual or suspicious. The caretaker's cottage, they reported, was in total darkness – the occupants were either already in bed or had gone out. Meanwhile a close check of the children's dormitory by the women confirmed all their junior charges were asleep.

Don and Sylvia joined Paul and Maureen, each armed with a torch, for a tour inside the old hospital. It was agreed amongst them that no light switches were to be turned on in case it attracted the attention of the caretaker – either from his bedroom, or if he returned home. Obviously, they fully recognized they were trespassing in an area forbidden to them.

Reaching the top of the stairs they checked and saw the door to the Dying Room was securely padlocked. On entering the dormitory they observed the door of the small inner room was locked too.

They moved to the fireplace. Each of the four torches immediately went out. As soon as they moved away, their torches came back on again. Don and Sylvia were dumfounded. The whole thing simply defied logical explanation. They moved towards the fireplace again. And again their torches failed; they moved away, and their torches came back on. They repeated the experiment three times, always with the same result.

A startling new experience was just moments away ...

As the group moved towards a small bathroom at the end of the dormitory, they heard the sounds of running water. Four torch beams shone from the doorway onto a washbasin illuminating hot water gurgling down the plughole! Both taps were hard 'off'. The hot tap was just that – hot to the touch!

It was implausible that anyone/anything could have left the room without being seen by the group. There was no other exit.

Stunned and scared as they were, they were not about to quit their hunt. In whispered conversation, they agreed to check every possible hiding place in the dormitory. They looked into every wardrobe, checked in and under every bed, and opened every cupboard. Nothing / nobody was found.

The foul smell was ever-present, only this time it seemed to move around the dormitory and was not concentrated in any particular place.

> On the way back they looked into the side dormitory and noticed a strange oblong shape in the middle of the floor. Thinking it may have been a shadow they switched on the light but it was not a shadow, rather it appeared as a small cloud of dark vapour which slowly dissolved as they watched. [Miriam Howard-Wright, 'Holiday Nightmare', Artlook Magazine, April 1980]

Convinced they had searched all possible hiding places, the group were about to retreat downstairs for supper, when they noticed what appeared to be light coming from under the door leading to the attic.

They had checked this door earlier and found it padlocked shut. Now the door was unlocked. As they approached, the light dissipated. They found no-one inside.

The four intrepid investigators continued downstairs for supper, trusting the others had nothing startling to impart. They had regularly checked the children and found them all fast asleep each time.

The adults took their cups and plates into the more-comfortable sitting room and listened to the accounts of the upstairs search party, leaving the torches on the kitchen bench. Then another weird thing happened ...

Everybody heard it. The kitchen door closed. It didn't just close, it was locked as well. Not only were their torches locked inside, but the caretaker had the only key to re-open it!

> They all sat there for a few minutes debating what to do when suddenly a tremendous noise or explosion shook the building. Joan's first thought was that the hot-water system had exploded. Then everyone raced out of the building across to the annex. The children appeared to be sleeping quite peacefully and nothing seemed to have been disturbed.
>
> Looking outside they realized that they had left the lights on in the old building but not one of the adults would brave going back there. Without the torches they were not game to risk going anywhere. [Miriam Howard-Wright, EYEWITNESS Australian Ghosts, Artlook Publishers, Perth, 1980 p. 127]

That is, with the exception of Sylvia, the visitor from York. Her husband's car was right outside and, after a short discussion between them, she and Don woke their children, bundled them into the car and Sylvia drove home to their own beds. Any mother placed in the same predicament would have done so! Don stayed on to help guard the visitors.

By now it was only a few hours to daybreak, so the remaining adults began preparations of sleeping arrangements. When Joan and Paul went through the bedroom they found Maureen sitting on her bed 'in a trance' with her face unrecognizably distorted. She recovered from her strange disfigurement within moments, and nothing was said to her about it.

One parent (who we'll call 'Vinny') was sitting up in her bed and called out 'There's something at the window next to Joan's bed!' If there was something there, it had gone before Paul and his mother reached the window. 'Vinny' swore she'd seen a ghostly figure, and quickly pulled the blankets over her head.

Paul and Don rested on a mattress on the dormitory floor. Other parents gathered an odd assortment of weapons and placed them within arm's reach of where the slept—cricket bats, cricket stumps, and even an aerosol can of fly spray. Brooms and mops were again strategically placed across the doorways.

Unexpectedly, Maureen Cramer yelled out that there was something close to the door. Everyone sat up and looked in that direction. They saw nothing.

> Even as they watched, 'Vinny' started screaming and appeared to be fighting with herself. Suddenly she was shouting to them, 'Why didn't you help me?' They looked at her in astonishment.
>
> 'Well you must have heard me – I was screaming.' She held her throat. 'Didn't you see her? She had me by the throat. She tried to kill me.' [Miriam Howard-Wright, EYEWITNESS Australian Ghosts, Artlook Publishers, Perth, 1980 p. 128]

Joan Harrison suggested to 'Vinny' that she must have had a nightmare, which 'Vinny' vigorously denied. It wasn't a nightmare, she said, because she was fully awake; then she proved this by correctly repeating the conversations between the other parents.

They looked at 'Vinny's' throat and saw a bruise where 'Vinny' said she'd been grabbed. Most were surprised into silence by what they saw. They shuffled back to their own beds, privately trying to process the experience.

Exhaustion overtook them all, but nobody slept.

Then the music started.

Paul had set up his record player in the sitting room hours earlier and played just one record before turning his player off. Now it was playing that record again, loud enough to be distinctly heard in the annex!

Neither Paul or anyone else was prepared to go outside and enter the sitting room to turn it off. That task would have to wait until daylight.

Joan Harrison later told writer Miriam Howard-Wright of another series of incidents that night:

> Joan remembers sitting quietly on her bed beside the window. The curtain was closed. She remembers feeling drained of all feelings and does not have the slightest idea as to why she suddenly pulled the curtain aside to look out. She registered no emotion of any kind when she found herself face-to-face with the apparition ...a cloudy, almost a vaporiform, the size of an adult. She dropped the curtain back and sat, as she said, like a Zombie.

After a few seconds she lifted the curtain again. It was still there. Again she let the curtain drop. She sat there and waited, looking every now and again to see if it had gone away. She figured it would go and eventually it did. She wondered why she felt so numb, so unfeeling.

The more she thought about the whole chain of events the more detached she became. It was, she explained, a strange feeling of not being anything at all. [Miriam Howard-Wright, EYEWITNESS Australian Ghosts, Artlook Publishers, Perth, 1980 p. 128]

When day broke on Friday morning, very few of the adults had enjoyed much sleep. But a few surprises still awaited them – the kitchen door was found unlocked. Paul's record player was switched off. The record they'd heard playing during the night sat on the spindle with the needle arm on the side at rest.

No-one felt like discussing anything that happened overnight. They busied themselves packing clothes and cleaning up in preparation for the bus trip home. Friday was their final day at the Old York Hospital camp. For the adults, the prospect of going home was a great attraction.

As arranged previously, Mr Cramer, Maureen's husband, arrived to take them all back to Rockingham in the hired bus. Having come off night-shift before driving to York, he had intended to grab some sleep before undertaking the return journey.

But after hearing a few stories of the extra-curricular activities they'd endured, and then looking around the site himself, he agreed there was something unhealthy about the place. Departure plans were altered.

Instead, everyone moved to Sylvia and Don's home in York where Mr Cramer grabbed a few hours sleep before the Rockingham Little Athletics Club group re-boarded the bus and returned to their familiar (and un-spooky) homes – where door knobs didn't spin, jugs didn't drop unaided, curtains didn't hide ghosts, torches didn't flicker and the peace was undisturbed by moaning and wailing.

☼

[Privately owned]

17. A Ghostly Non-paying Guest

standing immediately behind him, a misty green shadow outline of a human figure wearing a dark cape!

Benjamin Franklin once said: 'Idle hands are the devil's playthings.' This may well have applied to six young entertainers staying at the George Hotel in St Kilda during 1966.

They were visiting Melbourne from interstate, and one evening, according to lead guitarist John Green, 'We cobbled together a Ouija board, using George Hotel stationery.'

Four of them – singers Jeff St John and Marty Rhone, and two members of Marty's backing group, *The Soul Agents*, Barry Kelly and John Green – sat around a table in the main lounge of their run-down suite of rooms and conducted a séance.

The Soul Agents drummer Roger Felice chose not to take part. He preferred to remain seated on the nearby couch, chatting with a young lady he'd met that day.

The lads agreed Marty should jot down the indicated letters. Each placed an outstretched forefinger on the upturned glass in the middle of the table. 'Relax, and don't push the glass,' Marty advised.

'You ask a question, Jeff,' someone suggested, and straight off Jeff asked 'Is there anyone here?'

GHOSTS DOWN UNDER

Barry Kelly, Jerry Dean, Marty Rhone (front), John Green, Roger Felice

Slowly, as if by magic or the focused power of several minds, the glass moved rapidly across the table and came to rest on the word 'YES'.

All four boys glanced at each other suspiciously. Who was moving the glass?

Jeff cleared his throat nervously. 'Do you ... um ... have a message for us?'

The glass started to move again. This time it slid slowly, touching the edge of the alphabetical letters as Barry called them out, making sure Marty didn't miss writing any down.

'H..V..D'

Then it stopped.

'What the &%#@ does that mean?' John asked impatiently. 'There's no such word. This is nonsense, I think I'll go and ....'

John was halfway out of his chair when the glass slowly resumed its slow movement.

U..N..D..R

'None of this makes any sense!' Marty spoke up, 'Ask it who's sending this message.'

St.Kilda, Victoria

Jeff obliged, and the glass started moving around the board' again.

The next letters to be nudged were 'G' and 'E'. It paused momentarily before adding 'L', 'D' and 'A'.

Then it stopped.

"G,E' and 'L,D,A' doesn't spell anything!' Marty moaned, looking at the others, hoping they might have made some sense of the message. They hadn't.

Noting the forefingers still resting on the glass edge, Jeff St John seized the initiative again, 'Tell me again, Who is this message from?' he asked impatiently.

This time the glass moved swiftly through the letters of 'G.E,L,D,A' again and stopped.

'Gelda?' Jeff repeated, 'Is it a woman's name? Gelda? I don't know any Gelda.'

'Me, neither,' John shrugged, looking at Marty who simply shook his head. Barry Kelly paused, thinking, before admitting 'Either do I. No, I don't know any Gelda.'

The girl quietly chatting with Roger instantly stopped talking, broke into loud hysterical shrieks, and hurriedly left the room in tears.

Roger followed her into the dormitory bedroom intending to offer her comfort, but also anxious to find out what was causing her such sudden distress.

What he learnt, and told his mates, was astounding!

Firstly, Roger's new friend was Dutch, having grown up in the Netherlands before migrating to Australia.:

> The spirit they had connected with was that of [her] long lost, childhood friend [Gelda] with whom she had been skating on a frozen river. The friend had fallen through thin ice and was taken by the current. The body was never recovered. [Jeff St. John, The Inside Outsider: The Jeff St.John Story, Starman Books, 2015, p.82]

She tearfully explained that magnetic power cables under the frozen river had probably served to pull her friend down when the ice broke. In other words, they had heaved (hvd) her under (undr)]

Suddenly, the message made sense.

Seeking further verification that they had contacted a genuine otherworldly spirit, they then placed their forefingers back on the upturned glass and asked a final question.

'Where did this happen?'

The glass slowly moved around the board and spelt out H. O. L. L. A. N. D.

Totally spooked the boys tossed their temporary Ouija board out. They'd had enough of dabbling with the spirit world, or the spirit world dabbling with them!

At least, they hoped so!

But it was not to be. Their frivolous antics may have awakened a more sinister force.

Essentially, there were two pop groups staying at The George at that time, both booked in by their manager, Nat Kipner of 'Spin Records' in Sydney.

Jeff St. John and his backing group, *The Id*, had rooms in the main part of the hotel, while Marty Rhone and his backing group, *The Soul Agents* (John Green, Roger Felice, Barry Kelly and Gerry Dean) had far less salubrious accommodation.

Although accessed by the George's main staircase and elevator, their suite was actually located in an older three-storey annex next door to the main hotel.

It consisted of one small bedroom with two tightly-squeezed, single beds and a rear-facing window, plus a large dormitory with three or four single beds, a bathroom, and a very large lounge with sliding doors accessing a balcony which overlooked Fitzroy Street.

Stairs outside their door led up to a securely locked room, but no other guests occupied this part of The George.

With peeling paint and faded carpets, it looked as if there hadn't been any guests there in the past decade. In fact, the building was earmarked for future demolition.

St.Kilda, Victoria

The annex is circled on the left of this 1960's photo

After the Ouija board scare, strange incidents began to occur.

The first of these happened late one night when, after a gig, Marty entered the elevator in the hotel's ground floor reception area. He was alone, yet as he stepped inside and before he had a chance to press the button, he distinctly heard a voice, a very matter-of-fact disembodied voice, say, 'Take it up, Joe.'

Marty stood frozen as the elevator doors closed and he was silently transported to the first floor. He exited promptly, determined to take the stairs from then on!

Marty later convinced himself it was simply his imagination, but an incident the following day made him think twice.

'Hey fellers, come and have a look at this!' he called. Marty, Barry and Roger, had been lounging on the beds in the dormintory bedroom, as a Beatles LP was playing in the adjoining lounge. When the music stopped, Marty went in to flip the record over. That's when he called the boys in.

'Come on, quick!' he urged the others, 'You've gotta see this!'

Barry and Roger appeared in the lounge and Marty excitedly pointed out what he was so excited about.

The needle hadn't returned to the 'rest' position when it finished playing the first side. Instead, it had moved back to the fourth track and was playing it again.

Silently!

'Oh god,' Marty whispered, 'Look at the name of that track!'

'Don't Bother Me!'

Instantly, each thought of the séance and looked at one another in amazement, minds racing.

Then followed a string of startled profanities, the equivalent of 'Blow me down,' 'Stone the crows!' and 'I'll be damned!' (substitute more colorful words of your own choice!)

Marty swore that he hadn't touched the arm or the player, which, knowing Marty, everyone accepted without question.

Was it a further message from 'the other side'? Were they being told to stop fooling with the occult? Was it just a coincidence? A freak accident? An electrical failure?

Or was it a fair dinkum, straight-up warning?

≈

The next unexpected incident related to the room upstairs. The unoccupied, securely locked room.

Despite the fact they knew the upstairs room was always locked, the lads often heard footsteps up there, particularly late at night ... the time when the mind plays tricks on people who are trying to sleep.

Barry had heard those noises. So had Gerry.

Marty had heard them too, but he dismissed any thought of them being supernatural. He knew there had to be a logical explanation for the footsteps.

'Cleaners!' he insisted.

One afternoon, he heard someone on the stairs, and a jiggling of keys. He quietly opened the door and looked up, trying to keep out of sight. A woman — presumably a cleaner — had her back to him and was trying various keys in the lock. He stood and watched as she found the right key, opened the squeaky door and disappeared inside.

Then Marty bounded up the stairs to have a peek. This was his chance to prove that the room was nothing more than a cleaners' changing room, and that footsteps up there meant absolutely nothing.

> 'It was creepy,' Marty later recalled, 'Big old wardrobes with two glass doors and tops like coffins were tilted back against the wall!' Broken cupboards, and side tables with missing drawers or broken legs stood drunkenly, covered in the dust of decades. Framed mirrors with their glass cracked or half missing, spider webs thick with age hanging over it all.'

It was The George's furniture graveyard. Some pieces were too good to throw out, but most had parts salvaged to keep other pieces in service. (In its prime, The George had 169 rooms, the largest outside the city of Melbourne.)

Later, Marty told the others what he'd seen and declared that they had nothing to worry about. The footsteps were made by the cleaners as they tidied up.

Everyone pretended to be relieved. Secretly, everyone wondered why cleaners would be tidying a furniture graveyard covered in cobwebs at 3am!

However, the 'furniture graveyard' hid more secrets than any of them guessed.

While in Melbourne, Marty celebrated his 18th birthday, and an impromptu party was arranged in the suite.

The tale of their séance became the main discussion between drinks, and Marty followed with his spooky experience in the elevator and the weird self-selected Beatles track.

One of the guests, a well-known radio dj, was having none of it. Annoyed they weren't believed, Roger mentioned the mysterious footsteps they all heard on their ceiling in the middle of the night.

'Rubbish,' the dj scoffed. 'Come on, then! Upstairs! Let's

have a look at this pesky ghost!'

'The door's always locked so you won't...' John began to explain, but a small group had already adjourned to the stairwell, most with drinks in hand.

Anything for a bit of fun!

They stood or sat on the stairs, chatting and watching with amusement as the dj stood on the landing, waiting, for his audience to settle.

'Let's go and meet this bloody ghost!' he smirked.

With a drink in one hand, he grabbed the doorknob with the other.

'Whack!' An unseen hand slapped his wrist.

He leapt back in horror and yelped loudly. Eyes wide with shock, he stumbled down the stairs, grabbed his coat, and ran down the next flight of stairs two at a time, through the lobby and out into the street.

He never again returned to the George Hotel.

≈

The biggest, scariest shock, though, was just days away.

One weekend, the girlfriends of Jeff St. John and Gerry Dean arrived from Sydney to spend a few days with their men.

The couples were granted exclusive use of the small bedroom, as it provided some privacy.

On the first night of their visit, the rest of *The Soul Agents* went off to see Max Merritt and the Meteors while Jeff and Gerry remained at the apartment with the girls.

Roger remembers that when the group returned to the George, and even before they put the key in the door, it flew open. Gerry stood in the doorway looking distraught. He was upset and visibly shaking. His girlfriend was almost hysterical.

'What the hell happened?' Roger asked as the others crowded around.

St.Kilda, Victoria

'We saw a .. a thing, a ghost ...in there,' Gerry pointed towards the small bedroom. 'It frightened the shite out of me ... out of all of us!'

The couples had been in bed, chatting and drinking, when Gerry got up to refill a glass of wine from a bottle resting on the mantelpiece over the old fireplace. There was a mirror above the mantle which reflected the wardrobe mirror on the opposite wall behind him.

As he filled the glass, Gerry glanced in the mirror and saw, standing immediately behind him, a misty green shadow outline of a human figure wearing a dark cape!

Gerry yelled at his girlfriend not to look. But — of course—she did, and she immediately started screaming!

Showing masterly self-control, Gerry didn't turn around. He walked backwards between the beds towards the light switch by the door, through the spot where the apparition stood. He said it felt cold and smelt musty as he moved through it.

It 'evaporated' on contact.

As soon as he reached the door and switched the light on, all four of them scrambled, into the main lounge room and put all the lights on. They sat there, shivering, no-one knowing what to say.

Finally, Gerry decided to report the matter to the front reception desk downstairs. He dragged on a pair of trousers, grabbed a jacket and opened the apartment door.

That's when he was confronted by the rest of *The Soul Agents* coming home from the concert.

They all adjourned to the lounge-room, chatting over the top of each other.

Was it a real ghost? Or were the mirrors playing tricks on them? No. At least two, and possibly three, of them had seen the menacing figure.

'Is this for real?' Roger asked Gerry.

'Look at her,' Gerry replied sharply, indicating his girlfriend, curled up under a rug, sitting on the sofa, sobbing, 'Do you think I'd do this as a trick?'

Was anyone game enough to go back into the bedroom? At the very least, they had to retrieve articles of clothing from the wardrobe.

Besides, if they didn't sleep there overnight, they'd have to sleep on the lounge-room floor.

Roger Felice and Marty Rhone stood to one side in whispered conversation. They reached a decision ...

They walked, a little apprehensively, back into the bedroom. The window was closed and the cheap tattered curtains were drawn across it. The beds were in disarray, testimony to the rapid departure of the occupants.

'Whoever you are,' Marty announced bravely, 'make yourself known.'

Both observed the sheer curtains ripple. The only window in the room was firmly closed.

Then, suddenly, terrifyingly, the wardrobe door flew wide open!

Marty later recalled that he and Roger had to literally climb over each other in their haste to vacate the room. No-one slept in there for the remainder of their stay.

≈

The following morning Marty asked the desk manager if anything strange had ever happened in their apartment.

'Oh, do you mean the ghost?' was his calm response.

He explained that a World War 1 sailor had either been murdered there or fell down the stairs and had broken his neck, and confessed that many had seen a green mist in that part of the building.

Roger also made a few enquiries among the staff. He learnt that many years ago, the front desk received a call from that room and the caller asked for something to be brought up. The bellboy took it up, but didn't return.

He was later found dead in the apartment's doorway,

halfway in, halfway out, with a broken neck.

Two different stories, both including broken necks, from two different eras. Then there's yet another one. According to an article in the *Truth* newspaper:

> Although others have scoffed at the idea of a ghost, The George's general manager. Mr Frank Sherren, says there has been enough evidence in the past years to back up the stories.
>
> Legend has it that a few days before Xmas of 1905, a young man booked into a room and refused to take part in the pub's pre-Christmas festivities.
>
> One morning his body was found hanging in the room. He had suicided.
>
> The management tried to hush up the tragedy and within a few days the room was barricaded.. [Truth, Melbourne, 22 January 1972]

The room was barricaded in 1905? Perhaps it had remained that way for over six decades until a group of young musicians needed accommodation for five people.

In 1971—five years after *The Soul Agents* visit—The George presented Art Luden's long-running striptease show 'Getcha Gearoff' (and hung a banner across its Fitzroy Street portico reading 'This Is The Show' with visual emphasis on the first letter of each word)

The star of the show was Janette, a single mother of 7-year-old Jason, who lived together in a cheap room at The George:

> 'While I perform, I leave Jason asleep and keep on popping upstairs to see how he is. This night I just closed the door, without locking it, leaving him fast asleep.
>
> After I finished my opening number, I checked and found the door locked. I thought Jason had got up and done it, so I left my vanity case containing personal things and make-up outside the door and went downstairs for a master key. I had left my key inside.
>
> When I returned my case was gone, the door was open, all the lights were on, and the shower was full on too.
>
> Jason was still fast asleep. It was really frightening. I woke him and asked him if he had turned on the shower but he didn't know

anything. My case was found next morning on the hotel office floor.' Janette is convinced that she and her son have been victims of the ghost. [Truth, Melbourne, 22 January 1972]

Marty Rhone and the Soul Agents may have been the first paying guests to stay in the George's haunted annex for six decades. Is it any wonder the lone ethereal inhabitant found a way to send them the message: 'Don't Bother Me'?

A few years after Marty and the Soul Agents' stay, that section of The George Hotel was closed to guests once again.

According to general manager Mr Frank Sherren:

... over the years there have been several sightings of the ghost, especially when people wandered into the section which was no longer used. [Truth, Melbourne, 22 January 1972]

In the same interview, Frank Sheridan, a former private investigator, told of a personal experience he had, after breaking down a boarded-up door leading to this disused section:

'A cloud of dust suddenly jumped up in front of me,' he said, '... the dust came straight toward me and even followed me down the stairs. And the noise! I heard thumps and bumps and a kind of whistle. It was eerie.'

Since that article was published, the George has undergone a total transformation. It has been completely gutted and rebuilt into substantial apartments with high ceilings, baltic floorboards and million dollar price tickets.

The haunted extension has long since been demolished.

There have been no further reports of ghostly non-paying guests.

☼

[Privately owned]

18. A Specter in Loincloth and Turban

'..she had seen a strange person in her room...'

Twenty kilometers (12.5 miles) south-west of Launceston, Tasmania stands historic Entally House, 'one of the oldest pioneer colonial homes in Australia,' with its strange and haunting background.

> Nestling in parkland on the banks of the South Esk River in the village of Hadspen... the house has both character and a fascinating history. Standing on rising ground, which shows it off to good advantage... and being a working homestead, there are substantial buildings to the rear. [Robert Wilson, A-Z of Australian Towns & Cities, (Weldon, 1989), p. 201]

The property was taken over by the quaintly-named Scenery Preservation Board, an instrument of the Tasmanian Government, extensively restored, and opened to the public in December, 1950.

Prior to this occurring:

> Various tenants complained of a 'spectre' in loincloth and turban. And a woman boarder, who knew nothing of the house's background, became hysterical after 'seeing' it one night. [The Argus (Melbourne), 5 January 1954, p. 24]

Michael Sharland, the initial secretary of the Scenery Preservation Board and keen ornithologist, wrote an article on 'Tasmanian Ghosts' for People magazine in 1960:

> The story of its ghost is vouched for by tenants who lived in Entally for a little time in 1947 and who now reside in Sydney. A young woman staying with the family at Entally said she felt tired and would go up to her room in the attic to rest.
>
> She hadn't been there long, however, before she hurried down and told the others she had seen a strange person in the room. She described a coloured man wearing the costume of an Indian.
>
> She said he had come into the room and stood beside the bed. When she spoke to him he vanished, [Michael Sharland in People, 12 October 1960]

A similar encounter is mentioned in a paranormal blog site:

> Entally is said to be haunted by the ghost of a turbaned Indian. It is said that if you are unlucky, and a woman, you may run into him on the stairs. As you make your way up the narrow flight of stairs, you will come to a part you will not be able to pass. The air will instantly chill, and then the turbaned Indian will materialise for a few seconds before disappearing again. [Ashley Hall in www.theparanormalguide.com/blog/entally-estate]

In their book, Ghostly Tales of Tasmania, Joan and Buck Emberg suggest Entally House is 'haunted by more than one ghost'.

They tell of a man who was riding his horse near the old homestead, when he fell off heavily, and was brought to Entally (in a wheelbarrow!).

> 'Whether he was already dead when he was wheeled to Entally is not known,' they write, 'Perhaps he died in the house. What we do know is that wheelbarrows of colonial times were much larger and longer than they are now!'

They introduce this evidence to potentially explain a 'puzzling noise' of a wheelbarrow being pushed across cobblestones heard by 'numerous people'.

> 'Many have been frightened by the sound, especially as there are no cobblestones and the gardener's wheelbarrow is locked in the shed.' [p.109]

There have been other eerie incidents at Entally House. On one occasion, Entally worker — Maryanne — was vacuuming a long corridor:

> When Maryanne sensed someone standing over her shoulder, she wasn't very surprised ... Not only could she feel the presence, she could see the shape of someone from the corner of her eye. Yet, when she turned to speak, the shape disappeared.
>
> A few weeks later she was again vacuuming. She had finished cleaning downstairs and was in the process of carrying the cleaner up to the second floor.
>
> While ascending the stairs, she distinctly felt two hands touch her firmly on the head. As she tried to take the next step, the touch became even stronger – she was forced to stop! When she looked around, no one was there! [Buck & Joan Emberg, Ghostly Takes of Tasmania, Regal, Launceston, 1991, p. 109-110]

Entally House has direct links with the very early history of Europeans in Australia. It was erected by Thomas Reiby, the first son of legendary Thomas & Mary Reiby who built a shipping network trading between Sydney and India, the islands of the Pacific and Bass Strait. They eventually owned twelve ships.

Mary Reiby had been transported to Sydney in 1792 for horse-stealing at the age of thirteen. She married Thomas Reiby, a young Irish seaman with the East India Co. in 1794, and together built a highly-successful enterprise.

In view of the fact that Entally House is said to be haunted by the ghost of a turbaned Indian, it's intriguing to note that on April 6th, 1811. the Sydney Gazette (6th April 1811). announced that Mary Reiby's husband died ...

> ... from a severe indisposition of several months, the origin of which he attributed to a coup-de-soleil [sun-stroke] when he was ship-wrecked off the Indian coast.

19. The Guyra Poltergeist

'she heard the reply, 'Yes, I am all right. I am in Heaven.'

In the second week of April 1921 a home in the tiny town of Guyra in northern New South Wales was under threat; so the locals rallied, guns drawn, to get rid of the pest forever.

It was not as easy to accomplish as they thought. The threat was not of this world.

Guyra is on the New England Highway, midway between Armidale and Glen Innes.

The house at the center of this account was an isolated, four-roomed weatherboard home occupied by William Bowen, his wife and three children, about half a mile (800 meters) east of the railway station.

> The first of a series of mystifying events occurred a week ago on Friday, when, according to her story, the girl [Bowen's daughter, aged 12] was chased by a man about 4 o'clock in the afternoon a quarter of a mile from her home.
>
> While she was running away from him he pelted her with stones. By the time she reached the house the man had disappeared. Nothing further occurred until after nightfall, when the family were alarmed by a fusillade of stones striking the house. [The Braidwood Review, 12 April 1921, p.5]

Guyra, N.S.W.

Mr Bowen contacted a neighbor and together they searched an area around the house seeking the offender, without success.

First thing the next morning Mr Bowen personally reported the matter to the local police. A plan was laid for two constables to visit Mr Bowen's home at dusk that evening.

No sooner had Constables Stennett and Taylor arrived and taken a quick look around when a window pane was smashed by a small object from outside the house (possibly a 'pea rifle bullet'). Again, a thorough search around the house proved fruitless. An even wider search through the surrounding scrub went unrewarded.

It was time to catch this fool before someone got seriously hurt.

The next evening the constables returned, supported by Sergeant Ridge and four civilians, who placed themselves around the perimeter of the dwelling – making it almost impossible for anyone to get near the house without being seen or heard. Shortly afterwards the sentries heard stones thudding against the house walls and roof, and started closing in, searching for the instigator.

None was found.

Their inability to identify who was making this attack on an innocent family was becoming embarrassing for the local police who resolved to return nightly until the culprit was caught. They stood guard again the next night – stones fell, but no one was caught.

> Last Monday night the party was augmented by ten civilians, several being armed with guns. The men were placed around the house carefully, and so well were they placed that the leader declared that he was pretty well satisfied that no disturbance would occur that night. He was wrong, however, for a little later a window almost in front of Sergeant Ridge and Mr M. Heagney, one of the watchers, was smashed. [The Braidwood Review, 12 April 1921, p.5]

But there was still more to come.

Another house window was soon heard to shatter. The

waiting watchers moved in, lanterns lit, rifles cocked, voices calling to each other. Nothing and no one was found to account for these mysterious stonings. Nothing at all.

Inside the Bowen home, two stones—one, the size of a half-brick—were found lying on a bed.

Within the next thirty minutes, at least a further 20 stones struck the house. No further searches were held that evening – if thirteen men in an armed cordon around the house couldn't detect the thrower, what use were further searches?

On the fifth night, Sergeant Ridge rallied even greater resources. He gathered 40 volunteers. On this occasion ...

> Sergeant Ridge had procured a powerful searchlight. The house and surrounding country were swept by the beam constantly.
>
> Despite all the preparation, stone-throwing began shortly before 7 o'clock. And about 30 raps on the walls of the house were heard. Another search was without result.
>
> The Bowen family, with one exception, are greatly worried by the attacks on their hitherto peaceful home. The exception is the daughter who was chased in the first instance. She is apparently undisturbed throughout, and exhibits none of the signs of fear that are occasionally shown by other members of the family. [The Braidwood Review, 12 April 1921, p.5]

Suspicion of the 12-year-old girl, Minnie Bowen, grew – the stones seemed to be thrown at her; whichever room she was in became the room under attack. Minnie was closely watched each evening and it was soon established she was not responsible for either the stone-throwing or the wall-rapping. When police put the entire Bowen family in a single room under guard, the stone-throwing continued.

On Thursday night, Minnie was removed from the house altogether, and over fifty police and civilians watched the house overnight. While she was absent, no stones were thrown.

Immediately after she was returned on Friday afternoon, the stone-throwing recommenced – even in daylight.

One of the policemen entered the house:

A constable sat on a bed in the room beside the girl [Minnie Bowen], and stones fell on the bed. [The Braidwood Review, 12 April 1921, p.5]

The news of a week's unexplained stone-throwing and wall-rapping at Guyra began attracting attention in both regional and capital city newspapers.

Glen Innes, 61kms (38 miles) north of Guyra, sent their local newspaperman down to investigate. He reported:

A section of the community confidently declare that the whole affair is supernatural and refuse to go near the house again. The majority, however, are assured that it is a joke, though absolutely at a loss to locate the perpetrators.

On Tuesday night Dr. Harris, the local medico, organized a party and proceeded to the house after 8 o'clock. Dr Harris himself closely watched the girl throughout the night, and watchers were posted in every room and at every window, while other sentries stood in selected positions. Only the doctor's chosen few were admitted to the inner circle of the sentry line, on the outskirts of which there were over 200 persons. [Glen Innes Examiner, 14 April 1921, p.4]

It was half-past 10 before Dr Harris called the vigil off. He came outside and swung his lantern from side to side – his pre-determined signal.

It had all been futile – no stones fell that night.

... from every nook and corner the sentries came. Some of the party took the matter good-humouredly; others muttered something about fools and warm beds, while others just said nothing ...

'We'll have another go,' announced the medico ...the announcement did not meet with an altogether spontaneous response.

Thus ended another night's vigil, the chief feature of which was close supervision over the inmates and interior of the house. [Glen Innes Examiner, 14 April 1921, p.4]

The Glen Innes reporter also made some interesting observations about the 12-year-old girl, Minnie Bowen, who he said was 'of only ordinary intelligence for her age, and is, if anything, inclined to be dull.'

GHOSTS DOWN UNDER

The Sydney Evening News provided details of another aspect of the 'Guyra ferment' in their edition of the same date:

> It is reported that a spiritualist from Uralla attended, and persuaded Mr Bowen's daughter, around whom the attacks are centered, to ask questions.
>
>> When the knocking commenced she reluctantly consented, and asked, 'Is that you, May?' meaning her sister who died some little time ago, when estranged from her parents. The girl then said she heard the reply, 'Yes, I am all right. I am in Heaven.'
>
> It is reported that the knockings then ceased. [Evening News Sydney, 14 April 1921, p.6]

But not for long ...

A peculiar situation was recorded at Bowen's home during the Sunday night 'watch'. About eighty people formed the picket around the house, and four men were sent inside to guard ('watch') Minnie after nightfall in her bedroom, which is on the house's northern side.

Around 7.00pm the sounds of heavy stones striking the bedroom wall were heard by practically everyone.

The bombardment continued for some time, and the girl was quietly removed in the dark to the kitchen, which is on the south side of the house. At once the attacks on the bedroom ceased and the kitchen was under fire.

> It was late in the evening when the noises finally ceased, and a further search of the whole neighbourhood left the situation entirely unchanged. [Evening News Sydney, 14 April 1921, p.6]

Widespread media interest continued to fan the Guyra-stones story. The Inspector-General of Police, Mr J Mitchell, was quoted in several papers saying he believed the incidents were 'due to the activities of a band of larrikins,' who would have to be stamped out. He was arranging to 'send further police to help out' at Guyra.

The Newcastle Morning Herald expanded on this:

> Extra police ... under the command of Superintendent Banks, chief of the northern district, whose headquarters are in Armidale, should help to find the people who are scaring local residents.

Mr Mitchell had a visit yesterday from a policeman stationed in the metropolitan area, who had lived in Guyra when a boy. According to him, the present strange happenings in that town were but a repetition of events which he himself had witnessed 15 years ago.

In this case, too, a girl of 12 had been the alleged cause of the ghostly attacks; but the residents and police discovered, after patient watching and waiting, that she and a male confederate outside the home were in league, and jointly responsible for the stone throwing...

After hearing these facts, Mr Mitchell recognized the value of the constable's experience, and ordered him to pack his bag and take the first train to Guyra. [Newcastle Morning Herald, 20 April 1921, p.6]

Levity and skepticism soon began appearing in the various newspaper reports:

About 50 men of Guyra, in pursuance of their regular entertainment, went out to the Bowen house [Goulburn Evening Penny Post, 21 April 1921, p.4]

Suddenly there came half a dozen terrific bumps on the side of the house. The men inside, who could see nothing, rushed out. The men outside, who could see nothing to account for the noise, rushed in. The noise ceased, and that was the end of the ghost for that night. [Goulburn Evening Penny Post, 21 April 1921, p.4]

Many of those present had since the commencement of the spookish manifestations been converted to spiritualism, but even they, in their young enthusiasm, had to acknowledge that the noise was not the gentle tapping of a spirit. It sounded, said Constable Taylor, just as if someone had put a pumpkin in a sugar bag, and was thumping the wall with it. [Goulburn Penny Post, 21 April 1921, p.4]

The Sydney Morning Herald, as some may have expected, played the story with a straight bat – no colorful journalism there, just the facts, m'am. In their edition of 22 April, they introduced a new investigator into the Guyra tale – an 'earnest, thoughtful investigator' from the South Sea islands, Mr H. J. Moors:

Guyra, in Mr Moors' calm opinion, is subject of a typical demonstration of Poltergeist. Of this he is convinced.

What, then, is Poltergeist? It is a German term for 'racketing spirit.' The term is applied to certain phenomena of an unexplained nature, such as movements of objects without traceable cause, and noises equally untraceable to their source. The phenomena are attributed to the action of a Geist, or spirit...

Mr Moors, in discussing the matter yesterday said the people of Guyra resented very strongly some of the reports which had gone out from the township concerning the affair, because of their ceaseless vigils and very exhaustive efforts to get to the bottom of the disturbances. [Sydney Morning Herald, 22 April 1921, p.10]

Mr Moors also reported a disturbance in another house 200 yards (183m.) away from the Bowens' on the first night of his visit to Guyra. Its windows were smashed and the house contents had been thrown outside. Mr Moors was convinced that this event was not caused by larrikins because of the closeness of the nearby 'armed camp' at Bowens'.

Shortly after this incident, police requested all volunteers and visitors attending the Bowens' home, in daylight or darkness, not to arm themselves in the interests of public safety.

Acting on the report, the Inspector-General of Police issued instructions that 'in future all acts of larrikinism must be promptly dealt with.'

The Northern Star in Lismore, N.S.W. summed it up in a single sentence:

The Guyra police have received special instructions to get busy and clear up the whole affair. [Northern Star (Lismore, NSW), 3 May 1921, p.6]

Another country newspaper added its own twist on this directive:

Now the Inspector-General of Police has issued sharp orders to the local John Hops [rhyming slang = Cops] to skip around and root out the nest of humorists who are keeping this farce going. [Cessnock Eagle and South Maitland Recorder, 6 May 1921]

Obviously both the press and the public were divided over the on-going Guyra 'stone throwing' saga and it was decided that Minnie Bowen who was either its cause or its object (depending on which side of the fence you stood) should be removed from the scene altogether.

Early in May, she traveled sixty-one kilometers (38 miles) to the safety of her grandmother's home at Church Street, Glen Innes.

All went well for Minnie ... for the first week!

Shortly after tea on Monday night noises were heard like stones bumping on walls. The neighbours made enquiries, and the police were sent for. Constable Stewart was sent along to investigate, and while he and several others who had arrived were walking around the house a stone hit the window of Alf Shelton's [Minnie's uncle who lived with his mother, her grandmother] bedroom, breaking a pane of glass and becoming entangled in the curtain.

This stone was of ordinary white metal, and was similar to many others on the footpath in front of the house. The constable kept a close watch, with Minnie inside the house, and while there heard four or five distinct sounds resembling knocks against iron at a distance, but he was not sure whether they emanated from inside or outside the house. [Maitland Daily Mercury, 11 May 1921, p.4]

On Wednesday, Minnie's mother arrived from Guyra to take the child home. Before they left, the local police Sergeant was called in and 'spoke plainly with the girl, telling her if she started her tricks here she would have to be sent away' [the inference may have been 'sent to an institution'].

The next press report, two days later from Glen Innes, had Minnie Bowen and her mother back home safely at Guyra, and a rather eye-catching headline:

MINNIE BOWEN FROM GUYRA

A £500 Guarantee Ready

Many Guyra people will not entertain the suggestion that the girl is responsible for the disturbances, and it is stated that there is a backer with £500 in Guyra to say that the girl is not responsible. Certain members of the police force in Guyra concur in that belief.
[Sunday Times, Sydney, 15 May 1921, p.2]

In other words, 'Prove that Minnie Bowen IS responsible and win yourself £500'. (Five hundred pounds is roughly equivalent to $1,000 in today's currency).

At that point, a month after it started, the 'Guyra Ghost' story lost its potency.

The newspapers lost interest and moved their attention to other matters.

Later that year (1921), a well-known Sydney actor, Mr John Cosgrove, made a film using the house, the Bowen family and Guyra residents as its drawcards. He called the movie 'The Guyra Ghost Mystery'. Unfortunately only a poster for the film remains in the Australian Sound and Film Archive.

The whereabouts of any copy of the film is unknown. Much like the cause of the initial disturbances at Guyra.

☼

20. Resident Ghost in Cell 45

*'The prison comes alive
with phantom bangs and ghostly clangs.'*

Over a hundred years ago, Cell 45 in the Old Geelong Gaol housed a felon with a huge anti-social attitude … he was domineering, brutally aggressive and, according to The Argus newspaper, 'one of the most violent of men.'

In life, Percy Ramage did not take kindly to anyone invading his personal space – even if that space was a small, cold prison cell. In death, he continued to be a threatening presence to all who may be brave enough to invade his territory. He is still protecting Cell 45 from intruders at the Old Geelong Gaol today.

Ramage was foul-mouthed, quick tempered, tall, and powerfully built.

Here's what else The Argus had to say about him:

It seems that Ramage had severely assaulted a fellow prisoner and had been told by the [prison] governor that he would be brought before the magistrates for his offence.

He begged not to be confined to his cell, and the governor allowed him out in one of the yards. There he misbehaved himself again, and he was ordered to be taken to his cell. While this was being done, Ramage broke away from his keepers, and knocking down another prisoner, secured an axe, with which he defied the warders for some time [The Argus, Melbourne, 15 January 1902. p.5]

In the first three years of his incarceration at Geelong, Percy Ramage had been brought before the visiting magistrate charged with breaches of prison discipline no less than 15 times.

The Argus also disclosed why Percy Ramage was sent to gaol in the first place:

> His offence was that of battering Constable Luke over the head with a beer bottle. The bottle had shattered, and a piece of glass entered the eye of another man ... for a time Constable Luke lay in hospital between life and death...
>
> [Ramage] was sentenced to five years imprisonment with hard labour, a flogging of 15 lashes, and eight weeks solitary confinement. [The Argus, 15 January 1902. p.5]

Even today, more than a 100 years later, ghost tourists, ghost hunters and TV ghost shows often feel the brunt of Percy Ramage's spirit in Cell 45, Old Geelong Gaol.

> Cell 45 is the most haunted of all the cells in the prison, and many attendees have admitted to being pinched and even pushed into the cell. [Forte magazine (online), 11 July 2016]

Paranormal investigators Bill & Amanda Tabone and their adult, psychically sensitive, daughter Emily, had their first run-in with Percy in 2011 during an overnight examination, with others, at the Old Geelong Gaol:

> Staff members at the gaol told stories of seeing a black figure of a man [a shadow person] guarding the cell from the outside. During our time in the gaol we did not see any figures standing outside that cell, but we did have several altercations with 'The Man From Cell 45.'
>
> When we pulled out the Frank's Box*, a favoured tool on investigations, one of the first things we heard, after several minutes of listening and asking, was the phrase, 'F*** Off.' '[Emily Tabone, in Australian Paranormal Society, Facebook, 23 January 2011] * An electronic device, now known as a Frank's Box, created in 2002 by Frank Sumption. for real-time communication with the dead by capturing EVPs.

Geelong, Victoria

Later in the evening Emily and her father had to retrieve a camera they had positioned in a cell next to Percy Ramages' and Emily became aware of Ramage's hostile presence again.

I was very uneasy. The Man came closer, in a way which I describe as the 'Wanna go me?' manner—a real threat to intimidate [us]…I felt The Man come closer and I told Bill, 'He's right next to us!' I physically pulled Dad down the stairs.

I am not a strong girl, but I think I was so pumped full of adrenaline at the moment when The Man was ready to attack, that I forced Bill [with the camera] to the stairs. The Man backed off, and let us go. [Emily Tabone, in Australian Paranormal Society, Facebook, 23 January 2011]

More recently an international group, led by Robb Demarest of the USA, assembled for the 2016 TV series 'Haunting Australia' provided further insight into Ramage's character.

['Badboy'] Ian [Lawman] enters Cell 45 that over a hundred years ago housed one of Geelong's infamous inmates, Percy Ramage, a suicidally violent, giant of a man.

One night he tried to take his own life by cutting his neck, he screamed, two warders opened his cell and very quickly they shackled him. He was so big he managed to push his way passed two jail wardens, and [being] on the third level [of the gaol], he jumped for his life.

But Ramage got tangled on a cross bar, his shackles got wrapped around it and his arms were almost ripped from his body.

A stark reminder of this epic suicide attempt – the bend in the bar – is still there today. [Narrator, Haunting Australia, Series 1, Episode 2, 2016]

Twenty minutes of screen-time later, with Robb Demarest inside Cell 45, and Ian Lawman outside its closed door, Ian issues a brave challenge:

'Anybody out there who wants to, can come in here and 'Man Up' [fight]. Just walk into this cell.'

Robb was immediately aware of the sinister spirit of Percy Ramage in the cell with him, marking his territory.

I could see this dark mass raise up in the corner until it was six to seven feet [2m] high, towering over me.

Feeling threatened, Robb suggested to Ian that they swap positions, and Ian entered Cell 45, boldly calling:

'Righto, big guy, it's just you and I.'

Ian is still alone in Cell 45 with the seven foot tall shadow. The prison comes alive with phantom bangs and ghostly clangs.

Inside Cell 45, Ian seems to be facing off with a seven-foot tall shadow ...

Outside the cell, Robb has spotted yet another unexplained figure lurking near the gallows.

Ian left Cell 45 and staggered towards Robb. 'What happened?' asked Robb. 'I dunno,' Ian replied, 'you know when someone clutches your feet from behind. It was like that.'

Despite the use of night-cameras nothing specific made it to the screen. Some members of the 'Haunting Australia' team, however, were more successful in other areas of the gaol.

Among several other reported Old Geelong Gaol ghosts, there is a former prison guard who, 'rather than resting in peace, still patrols the prison in death'. He appeared unexpectedly to a local prison tour guide once and scared him enough for him to run out the premises:

> Just as I was about to leave, I looked up to the third level of the gaol and I could see the perfect silhouette of a man looking down at me.
>
> It was enough for me to feel so uncomfortable that I had to leave the building quickly. [Un-named tour guide, Haunting Australia, Series 1, Episode 2, 2016]

It is likely that the warder was the same person captured on Gaurav Tiwari's full-spectrum camera during the 'Haunting Australia' team's night-time visit in 2016.

> I was challenging the spirits to show themselves, to see if I could capture something [on film]. Zooming in, we discovered someone or something was definitely lurking in the dark. I can definitely make out the [profile] shape of someone standing and looking straight ahead – a full-bodied apparition! [Indian metaphysicist, Rev. Gaurav Tiwarii, in Haunting Australia, Series 1, Episode 2, 2016]

Geelong, Victoria

Other guides, who may seem quiet and assured, can get frightened, too. Geelong guide Jodi Hema was with a group in the prison kitchen when she was personally confronted.

'I was standing at the end of a table there one night, when I heard a noise to my right. I felt groping up my legs, all the way. It was invasive and scary. I actually ran out of the room screaming.'

In the 1860s and 1870s a wing of the Geelong Gaol became an industrial school for orphaned girls. One of their number, who looks like she's about twelve-years-old, is the most reported apparition seen in the building today.

Often sitting about halfway up the stairs, she looks sad and lost. She is attired in a ragged canvas dress and has long, matted hair. But if you feel like consoling her, she's gone before you can take a second step!

Site details: http://www.geelonggaol.org.au/

21. Shrieks in the Night

'eerie tappings on ceilings and floors'

Graham's Castle—also once known as Prospect House—laid claim to a number of ghosts in its heyday. There was talk of a headless man, sightings of a woman in white who tapped on the window, and another woman in black who strongly resembled the occupant's living mother.

There were also reports of eerie tappings on ceilings and floors and blood-curdling shrieks in the night! Some resident specters even arrived in a horse-drawn carriage which was heard coming up the gravel drive but never reaching the front door!

The mansion was originally named Prospect House by John Richman, who arrived in Adelaide in 1838 with his wife, four children, two maids and twelve workmen and their families. He purchased land on the corner of Prospect Road and Clifton Street, Prospect village and erected the 30-room two-storey house. It seems Richman was precisely what his name suggests, as he spared no expense ...

> ... rooms were spacious and opulent, with oak and cedar paneling and marble inlays. Some special features were a wide hall, a dining room with eight doors that fitted into recesses in the walls, and a paneled partition that could be folded back to turn two large rooms into a huge one.

A high stone wall surrounded the property, capped with broken glass to keep out unwelcome visitors. For those who were welcome, a wide drive ran through the grounds to a massive front door adorned with two cast lions' heads as knockers. All indigenous trees in the grounds were replaced with exotic ones planted in a formal pattern ...[David Johnson, Lost Prospect, Adelaide, 2014, pps. 21-22]

Richman even installed a pipe organ, the first of its kind in South Australia!

Eight years later, in 1846, Prospect House was sold.

The purchaser, John Benjamin Graham had left England and sailed for Adelaide in 1839 and within six years had accumulated a fortune as a result of shrewd investments in a copper ore mine. He purchased Prospect House for £400 and set about acquiring 52 acres of surrounding land.

Graham had become well known in financial circles, so businessmen and locals dubbed the property 'Graham's Castle' particularly as its crenulated parapet made it look a little like a 'castle.' It was a name that stuck.

Graham did not live in his 'castle' long. He returned to Europe in the early fifties and subsequently the house changed hands many times ... it was during the tenancy of Nathaniel Oldham that it acquired, rather after the fashion of stately mansions of the period, the reputation of being haunted. [Frank Cusack, Australian Ghost Stories, Melbourne, 1967, pps. 66-67]

The earliest of the ghost stories at Graham's Castle are difficult to confirm; particularly the one of the 'headless ghost' which was supposedly seen a number of times on the stairs leading to the roof. Legend has it that a man had hanged himself on the roof, but without a date or name one has to wonder if this was merely the chit-chat of servant's trying to frighten each other.

Far more reliable are the spooky claims of members of the Oldham family, who leased Graham's Castle in the 1860s.

Nathaniel Oldham's son grew up in Graham's Castle and was quoted in a lengthy article titled 'Ghosts of Early Adelaide,' published in Adelaide newspaper, The Advertiser, more than sixty years after the event:

> Mr G F Oldham, broker of King William-street, remembers well the ghostly reputation of the house when he was a boy and his family was in residence there for some years prior to 1866.
>
> ... Mr Oldham maintains that he recollects quite distinctly that one evening, about dusk, he entered the house and walked up the stairs. On the landing of the first floor he saw his mother in a black dress. He called out to her and ran to her room, but she was not there.
>
> That was not so strange, as at the time she was out driving.
>
> Another night, his stepbrother, who was about 15 years his senior, saw his stepmother standing in his room.
>
> 'Nothing in the world would ever persuade me that it was not my mother I saw.' Mr Oldham affirms.
>
> The servants stoutly maintained at the time that the house was haunted, and none of them ever stayed very long. It was an extremely difficult matter even to get servants for the house, let alone keep them. [The Advertiser, Adelaide, 17 October 1929, p. 19]

Six weeks later the Adelaide Mail ran a feature story 'Weird Hauntings of Early Adelaide' and included much of Oldham's recollections of the Graham's Castle hauntings.

The article ended with the following paragraph ...

> Some time later the family moved to Mitcham and the house was left empty. Years passed and rats and vermin became the only tenants of the place, its ghostly reputation had become known far and wide, and few persons would venture near the place after dark.
> [extract from Malcolm R Afford, 'Weird Hauntings of Early Adelaide', Adelaide Mail, 28 December 1929]

According to David Johnson, author of *Lost Prospect'*, other unexplained phenomenon were attributed to Graham's Castle during the 1880s:

> A story began that a woman had been murdered there ... It was said that a woman in white tapped on a window while a card game was in progress, only to disappear and be followed minutes later by a tapping of shoes on the stairs.
>
> Numerous different strange sounds were heard like a carriage scrunching up the gravel drive, but never reaching the front door,

eerie tappings on ceilings and floors and shrieks in the night [David Johnson, Lost Prospect, Adelaide, 2014, pps. 22 – 23]

The old mansion was unoccupied for lengthy periods. Its once-manicured gardens gradually became overgrown and unattended. At one stage students of Whinham College boarded there.

In September 1901, Graham's Castle was sold once more. Sadly, it was to be the end for the grand old house. It was demolished, and the land was sub-divided.

Do the occupants of houses built on the site ever hear tapping sounds on their ceiling, or awaken in fright to shrieks in the night? Have any noticed the strange scrunch of carriage wheels on non-existent gravel drives or felt someone was watching through the window?

After all, where do resident ghosts go when the residence itself no longer exists?

☼

22. Phantom of a Different Opera

*'There's something really weird about that.
It's not of this earth!'*

On the evening of Saturday, 3rd of March 1888, in Melbourne's greatest playhouse – the Princess Theatre – the premiere local production of Gounod's popular opera Faust was about to conclude.

The packed house closely watched as the final scene reached its climax with the heroine, Marguerite, dead in her prison cell, and the devil, Metastophiles, descending triumphantly into Hades amid fire and smoke with his new prize, Dr Faustus, who'd sold his soul to the devil.

The show's producers – Messrs Williamson, Garner and Musgrove – had a special trapdoor mechanism built into the stage to achieve this spectacular 'descent into hell' with the show's two leading performers gradually 'disappearing' from view as Metastophiles' last notes were sung. It was all very melodramatic!

The audience burst into spontaneous applause and cheers of 'bravo' echoed around the theatre.

The previous five weeks of rehearsals were paying off. Melbourne loved their new Faust. It was, as The Argus put it, an 'unexpected success.'

Melbourne, Victoria

Quietly the cast lined up behind the final curtain. Once raised, the leading players and chorus bowed under a spotlight, and bowed some more, while the applause continued to rain down upon them from the well-satisfied audience.

But theatres deal in illusion and all was not quite as joyous as it appeared.

Below stage, lay an unconscious man dressed in a satanic costume.

It was Frederick Baker, a 38-year-old Englishman born in Italy. His stage name was 'Federici', and his role in Faust was the central character Metastophiles.

The audience saw nothing of this macabre scene as it all happened in the under-stage cellar.

Perhaps they briefly wondered why he had not taken a bow so they could lavish applause on him as well. Then again, maybe they did see him take his final bow.

The following Monday's The Argus explained:

[Federici, standing on the trap] having drawn Mr Leumane [Faust] on to the trap, the two gradually disappeared, but just as their shoulders were on a level with the stage, Mr Federici was seen to put out his hands and clutch the boards. From the stage, however, nothing more was noticed. The trap ... has an oblique movement downward.

The fall is very slow and even ...Mr Federici stood, whilst Mr Leumane knelt beside him. As they disappeared, a red limelight was thrown on them from above. ['Shocking Occurrence at the Princess Theatre', The Argus, 5 March 1888, p.8]

Before the trap had mechanically reached the bottom of its drop, Federici fell and, grabbing Mr Leumane to steady himself, pulled him off the trap with him. They fell perhaps 45cms (18') and Mr Leumane rose to his feet unaided and scurried upstairs to take his bows with the rest of the cast, unaware that Federici lay unconscious in the dimly lit cellar.

On passing through the orchestra door below the stage Mr Alfred Cellier, the conductor, saw Federici lying prone and attendants trying to revive him. He ordered them to carry Federici to the green-room and place him on a mattress and pillow there. Meanwhile he sent messengers to find producer George Musgrove.

Federici's wife was also in the Faust cast; using her stage name Miss L Monmouth. She went quickly to the green-room to be at his side. Someone was sent to locate Dr Willmott, Federici's physician.

Dr Willmott, on his arrival, saw at once the seriousness of Mr Federici's condition, and having detected a slight beating heart, applied restoratives, principally the galvanic battery, at first mildly and then with increasing force, and while these were in progress, the patient died...

Dr Willmott had been attending Mr Federici almost since his arrival in this colony for affection of the heart, and prescribed for him nitro-glycerin pills, which is the most potent treatment for that ailment.

> Dr Willmott certified that death was the result of heart disease, thus obviating the necessity of an inquest. ['Shocking Occurrence at the Princess Theatre', The Argus, 5 March 1888, p.8]

The irony of the situation was not lost on those present:

> In the minds of all, the remembrance of the part played by the dying actor must have been uppermost, while the crimson hood, the pointed shoes and cap lying near him on the floor, could only seem a grim and ghastly mockery. [The Leader, Melbourne, 10 March 1888, p. 37]

The stage manager called the cast together to inform them of Federici's death.

Many of them refused to believe what they were told. They insisted Federici had been on stage with them to take his curtain call in his scarlet cloak and red silk tights. They swore to it and could not be persuaded from that belief.

The next day was Sunday, and the flag of the Princess Theatre was flown at half-mast. Speculation was rife among Melbourne's citizenry – who knew nothing of the unfortunate events of the previous evening. Why was the theatre's flag at half-mast? Who had died?

Melbourne, Victoria

Some believed it was Nellie Stewart. Nellie, Australian-born darling of the stage and long-term 'friend' of producer George Musgrove, sang her first grand opera part in Faust as Marguerite the imprisoned heroine. In her autobiography she wrote:

> By a strange coincidence, I, who had never had to do a back fall on the stage, was called upon to do so on that fateful night. When Marguerite died, my fall was so badly managed that I came down on the back of my head, with a fearful crash, which was heard all over the theatre.
>
> The next day was Sunday, and the flag of the Princess's being flown half-mast for poor Federici's death, it was thought by some that it was I, not he who had died. [Nellie Stewart, My Life's Story, Sydney, 1923 pps.95-96]

Monday's performance was cancelled as a further mark of respect; instead it became the day of Federici's funeral (and that had its complications as well!).

The procession moved from the deceased's place of residence in Grey Street, East Melbourne, at 2 o'clock. Its route passed the Princess Theatre, then took a direct course to the Melbourne General Cemetery, where the remains were interred.

> Mr. Alfred Collier, who was an old friend of the deceased gentleman, led Mrs. Federici to the grave. The Rev. J. H. Goodwin, chaplain of the cemetery, attended for the purpose of reading the burial service, but just as the coffin was being lowered he was seized with a fainting fit, and had to be carried away. [The Leader, Melbourne, 10 March 1888, p. 37]

Mr Charles Warner, a well-known actor who was present, was invited to take up the reading, which he did 'in a voice full of emotion' (according to The Leader). The burial was completed without further disruption.

> Faust folded within weeks. As a writer for Illustrated Australian News succinctly put it: 'The venture proved somewhat unfortunate ...[Federici's] substitute was not up to the mark.' But if the stories are correct, one cast member lingered on after the production wrapped. [Nellie Stewart, My Life's Story, Sydney, 1923]

That one lingering cast member was Federici himself.

Numerous 'Federici' sightings have been reported since 1888 – sometimes he is in full evening dress, sitting quietly in the dress circle observing the action on the stage – usually during rehearsals. At other times his presence is detected or felt rather than seen. He is also believed to be the instigator of items moving from one place to another within the theatre – 'his little bit of fun.'

The Princess Theatre, Melbourne

Here are a few selected examples of staff and performers who have reported seeing Federici at the Princess Theatre, Melbourne or believe they felt his presence:

One of the early possible sightings took place not long after the show closed. George Musgrove, one of the producers involved in staging Faust, saw a man seated in the dress circle late one evening during rehearsal. He chastised his staff for allowing someone into the theatre. An upstairs search was instigated, but the visitor had vanished.

In 1917, a fireman doing his rounds at 2.30am, and knowing the theatre's wardrobe mistress was working back, knocked on her door.

> 'Excuse me, Miss Beddoes,' he said, 'er … would you like to see a ghost?' Curious but sceptical Betty said she would and followed the fireman up the side stairs to a landing beside the dress circle. The fireman pointed. Betty looked and could not believe her eyes. Federici was sitting in the middle of the second row of the dress circle, quite motionless and staring down at an empty stage … The wardrobe mistress and the fireman watched the spectre for a long time and it was still there when they returned to work. [Richard

Davis, Great Australian Ghost Stories, Sydney, 2000, p.21]

[Another] Fireman John Gange twice saw Federici while making routine late-night checks of the theatre. The ghost was tall and handsome with a touch of distinguished grey at the temples and appeared quite real – up to the moment when he slowly faded away before the fireman's eyes. [Jane Sullivan, 'Haunting Tales, The Age, Melbourne, 16 April 1981, p.39]

June Bronhill reprised her highly successful West End role in the musical Robert and Elizabeth when it opened at the Princess Theatre, Melbourne in May 1966. During one performance she saw an unusual light moving about behind the rear seats of the dress circle.

'It was very strange, glowing in the center and dull around the edge, with a sort of pinkish tinge to it. It moved slowly backwards and forwards for three or four minutes then suddenly ... it was gone.'

Did she think she had seen Federici? 'I'm not sure. Someone told me he died in a red costume, so maybe the pink colour is a faded version of that. I really don't know what I saw and certainly not who I saw, but I do know I saw it ...and I looked for it every night after that.' [Richard Davis, Great Australian Ghost Stories, Sydney, 2000, p.22]

Rob Guest played the lead role in two outstanding Australian productions at the Princess Theatre—as Jean Valjean in Les Miserables, and as the Phantom in Phantom of the Opera (he ultimately performed the Phantom a world-record 2,289 times!).

'When I was doing Les Mis, I was backstage about to come on for the barricade scene, when I was supposedly seen at the back of the dress circle by one of the ushers. She went over to ask was there a problem, but was distracted by somebody else, and when she looked back, I'd gone. But, of course, it wasn't me. And I just thought maybe it was Federici himself who had taken on the persona of the lead character in the show. [Rob Guest on Rewind (Justin Murphy, compere), ABC TV, August 2004]

Trina Dimovska had a closer encounter at the Princess Theatre, where she worked as a cleaner:

'I felt something bad behind me – it just touched my hair and shoulders, and the back of my body. I just froze, because no one was there – no human. I was by myself because the theatre was closed. I started to sweat, because I was terrified...(laughs) ... Now I believe we have a ghost in this theatre,' [Trina Dimovska on Rewind (Justin Murphy, compere), ABC TV, August 2004]

Caroline O'Connor played Anita in the 1994 national tour of West Side Story. An unconfirmed story says Caroline saw Federici sitting on a garbage bin set on the edge of the stage during rehearsals.

Elaine Marriner, executive director the Princess Theatre, has personally witnessed several unexplained, out-of-the-ordinary incidents. Once she was showing some visitors around the theatre after hours:

'There are no windows. No light can come into a theatre auditorium. And when we were having a look at the theatre auditorium and stage, we actually saw a shaft of light come onto the stage. It didn't sort of register with us until later, how it could it have happened? Other than perhaps our friend Federici was making his presence felt?' [Julie Miller, Something is Out There, Sydney, 2010, p.91]

'Last year (1996), she had her own brush with the ghost. She and a friend were walking in the dress circle and all the seats were up. 'My friend said she felt something brush past her,' Marriner recalls, 'When we looked down the row again, one of the seats was down. And they don't stay down unless someone is sitting in them.' [Who Weekly, 10 June 1996, p.60]

Opera singer Morag Beaton felt Federici's chilling presence when rehearsing Turandot. She had not heard of Federici then, but she recognized the feeling – it was just like that shivery sensation she got in a cottage where a witch had been stoned to death. [Jane Sullivan, 'Haunting Tales, The Age, 16 April 1981, p.39]

Michael Cormick, as the 'Beast' in Beauty and the Beast in the Jacobson/Edgely long-running production at the Princess Theatre (1995), has two Federici tales to relate:

'I was surprised just how easy it was to become the 'beast'—but it did take about three hours to adorn the make-up and costume. I would go into a meditative state...I'm sure Federici visited me during these periods of deep relaxation. Many times I'd jolt back to consciousness and wonder who was there with me. There wasn't anyone ... but I felt there was a definite presence.'

Melbourne, Victoria

While singing a solo during the show, Michael Cormick was aware of someone humming along with him during the number. When he questioned other cast members, he learnt that if Federici enjoyed the rendition, he would join in by humming along with the soloist. No one else could hear it, but Michael knew he was attracting ghostly approval.

Rachel Beck starred as 'Belle' in the Jacobson/Edgely production of Beauty and the Beast at the Princess (1995). Initially a non-believer when it came to ghosts, Rachel soon changed her 'tune' while 'teching' (sound levels, lights, movement) the song 'Home':

> 'I actually saw Federici! I saw the ghost!' Rachel told us. 'I turned around and he was sitting in the middle section of the Princess Theatre, with a white hat and white suit, with his elbows together, just slowly clapping. I didn't know he's actually known to dress in white! He had a white glow about him.
>
> I thought 'Oh, what's that?'
>
> When I turned back again he was still there, slow motion clapping. 'There's something really weird about that ,' she thought. 'It's not of this earth!'
>
> My friend Danielle Barnes and a couple of other understudies were watching from up there and I asked 'Was there someone really weird up there? Has someone been let in to watch the tech?'
>
> They said 'Oh, no, no-one was up there.'
>
> Rachel recalled: 'My eyes started watering and the hairs on my arms stood on end, and I thought: Oh, my goodness! I've seen Federici! I'll always remember it.'

The lyrics Rachel was 'teching' at the time may have been particularly significant to Federici as it's a poignant song about home being where the heart is.

Blair Edgar, co-founder of Melbourne's Green Room Awards, was working on-stage at the Princess Theatre with Malcolm Lewis, director, when he was introduced to Federici's ghost:

> 'Malcolm was looking out into the theatre, and he said 'There he is, the poor old bastard,' and I said 'Who?' He replied 'Fed, he is out there in the Circle.'...I turned around, and there he was, up there in the Circle. The theatre had gone cold; and I became conscious of a strange lavender-type smell.
>
> What we saw was a shape of white light, with a diffused grey light around it. All I can say is that's what happened to me, right here on this stage and whatever it was, was up there' (pointing to the Dress Circle). [Blair Edgar in Haunted, TV series, with Dr Maurice Marsh, UNE, 1989 (part 7)]

Federici's presence is regarded by theatre management as 'a blessing' – any talk of exorcism is quickly shut down. Prior to a change of ownership and extensive renovation in 1987, a third-row dress circle seat was always kept vacant in the ticket office for his exclusive use.

23. Ghostly Hotspot

'...it materialized into a woman in a long, flowing white dress'

Picton is a picturesque town in the Wollondilly Shire, about 80kms south-west of Sydney. It has parks and gardens, original nineteenth-century buildings, a lookout with panoramic views and a picturesque suspension bridge 5kms out of town.

It also has a reputation as 'Australia's Most Haunted Town', and with good reason!

Paranormal writers Julie Miller and Grant Osborne, agree:

> Picton's reputation as 'most haunted' may be due to documentation and a thoroughly researched history, but having experienced more spooky goings-on in one single evening than we have in years of ghosthunting, we believe Picton's paranormal crown is well-deserved. [Miller & Osborn, Something is Out There, Sydney, 2010, p. 30]

The reference to 'thoroughly researched history' is an accolade probably intended for the late Liz Vincent who wrote and published some 20 local history works, including references to apparitions and unexplained phenomena. Due to the interest in this aspect of Picton, she decided to organize a ghost tour in 1997.

GHOSTS DOWN UNDER

It booked out within hours.

Liz then ran regular tours of Picton's paranormal hotspots until her untimely death in 2009. Her husband John continued the tours, but had to cease them in 2011 after facing development approval issues with Wollondilly Council. [Tim the Yowie Man, Haunted & Mysterious Australia, Sydney, 2017, p. 38]

Since 1819, Picton (then known as Stonequarry) had been an important stop-over during road journeys between the country's two most populous cities—Sydney and Melbourne. Today, however, the train and busy Hume Motorway both by-pass the once-thriving township.

Picton is now a quiet rural township with a population of around 5,000 living people.

Of course, no-one knows for sure how many NON-living residents chose to remain.

Dozens of ghostly appearances are regularly reported in various locations in the area. A few of these are known by name, others by occupation. Some are quiet, others menacing. Some are heard, and some are seen.

At the old Maternity Home (now a private residence), sounds of crying babies have been heard when none were nearby. The presence of a grumpy, no-nonsense matron has also been reported. Overnight visitors have occasionally been awakened from their sleep by invisible hands around their throat.

The Wollondilly Shire Hall, originally built as a school in the early years of last century and extensively renovated since, is now a history museum, function room and theatre. It has three resident ghosts. The Picton Theatre Group report that Ted, a bearded, non-ticket-buying presence, stands in the furthermost corner from the stage as a critic, wearing his hat and suit (shades of Federici!].

Another specter is heard crying during rehearsals. Locals believe these sounds are made by a young girl hiding under the stage, but none have seen her. A small, unknown but mischievous lad has also made his occasional presence felt by running across the Shire Hall stage.

Picton, N.S.W.

The Pioneer Graveyard dates back to the 1850's and is situated beside St Mark's Church in Lower Picton. Both are surrounded by homes today; and some cemetery visitors and locals walking nearby report hearing children laughing and seeing a young boy and girl holding hands, walking between the headstones and then just disappearing.

In January 2010, a cemetery visitor snapped a photograph of the pair, which was widely published in newspapers. It is believed locally that the lad was David Shaw who died from polio in 1946 (the son of the minister), and the girl was Blanche Moon, who died 124 years earlier after a pile of railway sleepers she was playing on slipped and crushed her to death.

The photographer, Renee English, swore there were no children at the cemetery when the photo was taken, and the pair was only seen after the image was downloaded to her computer.

Then there's Picton's Imperial Hotel—the haunt of many a ghost. It was originally licensed in 1863 as the Terminus Hotel, but in 1877 Colonel John Hay Goodlet bought it for an entirely different purpose. It was to become a sanatorium, a home for tuberculosis sufferers. The sick and dying were brought to Picton by train, and taken into the Terminus through a tunnel that linked the station with the hotel cellar. Many patients died lingering deaths in the building.

Although the old hotel is no longer a sanitorium (it reverted to being a hotel in the 1880s and was renamed The Imperial) it would seem that many patients chose to remain. Eerie incidents occur regularly. Workers say they often feel someone looking over their shoulder, but when they turn to look, no-one is there. Hard-to-close doors slam shut after staff walk through the doorway, and upstairs windows appear to have curtains being drawn when there are no curtains at all!

Then again, perhaps the invisible residents at the Imperial are actually past customers of the old 19th century Terminus Hotel, as the jukebox had been known to start playing even though it's disconnected from power!

The Emmett Cottages are a series of old semi-attached buildings where shop-owners often find their merchandise displays altered or moved around overnight. Should shop-keepers put things back how they want them, the mysterious overnight energy may rearrange them yet again!

The ghost of a woman is also seen occasionally in the window of one cottage.

Not far out of town is the Antill estate, now the home of Picton's golf course and the old homestead, 'Jarvisfield'. Built by John Macquarie Antill in 1864, 'Jarvisfield' is now the home of the Antill Park Golf Clubhouse. In the nearby cemetery—which 'Jarvisfield' overlooks—Major Antill and twelve close family members hopefully rest in peace.

Then again, perhaps not ...

> ... this is no ordinary clubhouse. It is, in fact, the original mansion of Picton, the former home of the pioneering Antill family. 'Jarvisfield'... is said to host several phantoms from the past, including a man dressed in period clothing nicknamed 'The Footman' and spirit children heard running around the second storey.
>
> ...two strange things happened which we witnessed – a door squeaks open of its own accord, and a bathroom light switches itself on. Faulty wiring? Crooked floorboards? Or very active entities? [Miller & Osborn, Something is Out There, Sydney, 2010, p. 30]

Viewed from surrounding parkland, the Railway Viaduct over Stonequarry Creek is a picturesque site located at the end of Webster Street. Built between 1863 and 1867, it has five massive arches and is the state's oldest stone archway. The middle arch is 78 feet high and was once used by local lads as a jumping off point to swim in Stonequarry Creek.

How many drowned there is not known, but if you sit very quietly, and listen very carefully, it is said that you may still hear their voices drifting towards you on the gentle breeze.

One remaining Picton ghost site appears to 'out-haunt' them all – the Redbank Range Railway Tunnel, sometimes called the Mushroom Tunnel.

Picton, N.S.W.

The Redbank Range Tunnel opened in 1867 and was used by trains until 1919. It was closed and empty until World War II when the Department of Air used it to store ammunition, mustard gas, and bombs. After the war it was used as a mushroom farm.
[Tim the Yowie Man, Haunted & Mysterious Australia, Sydney, 2017, p. 38]

Historically, the Redbank Range Tunnel was the first railway tunnel used by the New South Wales Railway, and is described as 'a fine example of the stonemasonry and tunnel design of its time.'

The Tunnel is relatively close to town, and some claimed unstable locals have suicided by jumping on to the track as the train emerged. This is possibly true, but dates and names are absent, as are death notices, obituaries and coroner reports of such instances.

For one outstanding case, though, we have full and startling evidence.

In 1916 a train from Thirlmere struck and killed a 51-year-old local, Miss Emily Bollard, in the Redbank Range Tunnel as it approached Picton station. Her obituary was published in the Picton Post on 20th December that year.

The Bollards had lived in Picton for half a century. Emily Bollard was taking a short-cut through the tunnel to visit one of her brothers when she was struck by the train. She was badly mutilated on impact, and subsequently found dead by a railway fettler about 11-metres in from the northern end of the tunnel. She was buried in the Upper Picton Cemetery in mid-December, 1916.

But Emily Bollard's spirit was reluctant to leave the district she grew up in – and the tunnel she died in – even though its now more than a century since her death.

Author Liz Vincent's husband John told documentary maker Erik Magnusson in 2010 that old Picton residents had seen Emily's ghost in the tunnel when they were playing there as children.

In one of her books, Liz Vincent provides an account of her first encounter with Emily Bollard's ghost in the Redbank Range Tunnel. (Liz was leading a ghost tour at the time):

> The atmosphere in the tunnel was positively charged ... As we watched, the white light flew down the left side of the tunnel and when it was about twenty feet [6m.] in front of us it materialized into a woman in a long, flowing white dress. We froze. All except the sceptic, who screamed, turned and ran. The rest of us watched as the woman floated down the right side of the tunnel and eased back into a distant white light. [Liz Vincent, Ghosts of Picton Past, Picton, 2004, pps. 64-65]

Visitors on different tunnel tours report other strange attributes of Emily's ghost: 'She is face-less,' 'Someone was patting my hair, but no-one was near me!' and 'I could feel a dark, negative energy field around me, I got very nauseous.'

One visitor, Danielle Formosa, recalled:

> 'While we were focusing on Emily, a big black shadow came right up to our faces ... When he breathed on me, it freaked me out ... frankly, it gave me the shivers' [from Erik Magnusson's video documentary]

Visitors to the tunnel have reported cold spots, and seen the white figure of a woman without a face, and they mention having feelings of great sadness. It is said that she sometimes will only show herself to one person in a group, and that these people have been so distressed by a feeling of terror that they have to be carried out of the tunnel depths. [Darnley Sullivan, Ghosts of Australia, Kindle ebook]

Picton, N.S.W.

Redbank Range tunnel is on private property and 'no trespassing' laws apply – seek permission before entering.

Even with permission, author Liz Vincent strongly urges ghost hunters not to tackle the tunnel on their own, warning that 'several people have had frightening experiences.'

There are several other published anecdotes about Picton, but locals are very protective of 'their ghosts' and are reluctant to discuss them with strangers.

Is it any wonder—when residents embrace their specters with such fondness and loyalty—that Picton has gained the reputation of being 'The Most Haunted Town in Australia'?

☼

Site details: http://visitwollondilly.com.au/visitor-information-centre

24. Don't Mess with 'Henry'

'Out of the darkness, an apparition appeared, almost like a fluorescent light...'

The Alkimos — a 7300-tonne freighter—was a floating disaster looking for somewhere to happen. And she found it. Regularly.

Some say she was jinxed. Perhaps they're right. Then again, maybe 'Henry' had something to do with her breakdowns, collisions, engine room leaks, mechanical and equipment failures, anchor chain snaps, on-board fires and groundings.

Who was 'Henry'? No one seems to know. He wasn't a member of the crew, nor was he a stow-away. The former chief steward of the Alkimos told skin diver and filmmaker Jack Sue that 'Henry' had been on board for a long time:

> I have never seen him, but I have listened many times during the nights to his footsteps climbing the ladder which stands on the deck above my bunk. The ladder goes up to the bridge. Many times I have investigated and seen nothing. Footsteps outside my cabin, too ... always nothing.

> Many times I have awakened in the middle of the night, wakened by the smell of cooking from my galley ... so I would investigate. And always I would find no one, and nothing disturbed. The cooking smells would go away as I opened the door.

The Alkimos was hastily built in Baltimore in 1943, intended for wartime crossings of the Atlantic supplying U.S. and Allied troops. She was sold off into private ownership before WWII ended.

When she ran aground on reefs off the Western Australia coast in 1963, she was equipped with modern navigational aids, yet she was eighty nautical miles off course!

How was that possible? Human error? Or ghostly interference?

Once freed, she caught fire while awaiting repairs in Fremantle. Then she suffered the indignity of being towed away towards Hong Kong, with no engine power of her own, only to have the towline snap in heavy seas. She then drifted until she became wedged on a reef.

A second attempt failed when the tug towing her was 'arrested' on behalf of the Bank of America. The Alkimos had to drop anchors and hope they held.

They didn't.

The Alkimos – almost defeated and totally exhausted – dragged her anchors to Eaglington Rocks off Yanchep. But if 'Henry' was to blame for her constant disasters, he was not done yet. Another snapped anchor chain sent her drifting until she beached herself a short distance off shore, wedging herself firmly on rocks.

It was then the fun really began!

To avoid Alkimos being declared abandoned, two Filipino crew members (Flora and Rufino) agreed to remain on board. Had they known that they were not to be the only residents of the ill-fated ship, perhaps they might have reconsidered volunteering!

Their experiences on board echoed the former chief steward's recollections. They were to have several close encounters with 'Henry', who became their unseen adversary. Tools they regularly used would suddenly go missing, only to reappear later in a different location. The pair also heard heavy footsteps following them at night.

As the chief steward had mentioned, cooking smells

came from the galley, along with sounds of pots and pans and the clash of dishes and plates. Cautiously, and always together, they'd quietly advance to the galley door and open it quickly, hoping to catch an intruder. It was always empty, and the smells were gone.

'Henry' was up to his tricks again!

On one occasion, Phil Krakouer – an experienced seaman and local recluse – agreed to go aboard to relieve the Filipino watchmen as temporary caretaker for a few days.

The Alkimos by this time was broken-backed and rusting, with the pungent smell of bird droppings permeating the hulk. Below deck thousands of rats had found their way into the grain cargo, and the stink of rat manure added to the awful stench.

By the feeble light of his torch and lantern, Ray Krakouer spread his bedding in the former Chief Steward's cabin, climbed the twisted stairs to the upper deck, lit a fire and cooked his evening meal.

The total darkness, the caw of the gulls, the limited circle of light from his lantern, the scampering rats, and the metallic groans of the slowly dying ship were poor dining companions for Ray Krakouer that night. He finished his meal, and feeling ill at ease, returned to his cabin.

He awoke to the faint sound of footsteps outside the cabin, but dismissed them as fanciful. Then he heard mumbling, guttural voices outside his door and leapt from his bed to investigate.

Quietly taking his lantern in one hand, Ray flung the door open with the other and stepped outside. Nothing. No one. And no more voices. Just more rats scurrying away from the light of his lantern. Baffled, he returned to his cabin, and locked the door.

Ray climbed into his bunk, but sleep would not come. He lay listening to the repetitive sounds of the Alkimos complaining – metal grinding against metal, pipes clanging against bulkheads, water slapping the ship's side, and the grinding shudder of a ship being swayed by the sea while wedged on rock.

Again and again the sounds repeated in a monotonous rhythm.

In the pale light of dawn he stepped outside and was pleased to see a few local cray boats in the vicinity checking their pots. They paid no heed to Alkimos's creaking hulk; they were accustomed to seeing her stuck there practically motionless as they went about their daily routines.

His day passed without noticeable incident, but not the following night ...

Around 9.30pm, Ray Krakouer lit his kerosene lantern and took a short pre-bedtime tour of inspection. He thought he heard footsteps following behind him; when he stopped to check, so did the footsteps. It was all in his mind, he told himself nervously ... safer, perhaps, not to think about them too much.

As he entered one of the cabins, the heavy door slammed shut behind him. The sound ricocheted with increasing intensity around the walls. Terrified, Ray fled the cabin, then tried to convince himself it must have been the wind playing tricks on him. Yes, it had to be the wind, didn't it? Or a movement of the ship perhaps, or ... or ...

Once back in his cabin Ray securely locked the door behind him. Again sleep eluded him for many hours; the usual groaning, grinding, shuddering sounds of the restless Alkimos were mixed with other sounds ... like pots and pans being thrown aggressively against the galley wall and heavy equipment being hauled back and forward across the deck.

And again, the footsteps, outside his cabin. Those bloody footsteps.... Invisible people can't make heavy footsteps, can they? Ray tried to think his way through it all. None of this is really happening is it? It all seems to be real, but it couldn't be, surely?

In the small hours of the morning, Ray Krakouer slipped into a light sleep. But even that was short lived!

A foul odor startled him awake. As he regained consciousness, Ray thought he heard those mumbling, guttural voices again. He tried to sit up. He was paralyzed, frozen stiff with fear. He felt as though he was being held down by a far greater force.

Had he been dreaming? Was this a nightmare? It was all so real, so disorienting!

Dazed and bewildered, he threw off the cloak of restriction and put his feet firmly on the deck. Thankfully, the foul smell had disappeared.

After breakfast, Ray busied himself on the open deck, replaying his recent experiences over and over in his mind. He was unable to accept the existence of ghosts or anything even slightly paranormal.

A further confrontation with 'Henry', however, was just hours away ...

During the afternoon, Ray Krakouer worked in Alkimos's cavernous No.2 Hold, breaking open a large box filled with copper cable. Timber and steel were scattered around his feet as he jemmied the crate open. Without warning, Ray's 'fight or flight' reflexes alerted him to a nearby danger:

> 'Out of the darkness, an apparition appeared, almost like a fluorescent light in the shape of a person,' Ray told Dr Maurice Marsh in his 1989 TV documentary, 'Haunted'. As it hovered in front of him, Ray grabbed a piece of 3" x 2" timber lying in the rubble at his feet, and prepared to defend himself.

'I was going for it,' Ray said, 'but the junk lying around was in my way; so I turned and went up the ladder.'

Discretion, the proverb says, is the better part of valor.

Fresh air and daylight helped Ray gather his composure. He was comforted with the knowledge that a friend was collecting him in the late afternoon, so he wouldn't have to spend another night on board Alkimos.

But 'Henry' still had another surprise to spring ...

Ray Krakouer didn't scare easily, but he found his experiences onboard Alkimos unsettling. There was something 'spooky,' un-nerving, and odd about her. He was relieved to be leaving her today.

While gathering his possessions together, Ray walked

Yanchep, West Australia

passed the Wireless Cabin which was sealed by a padlocked door. To his amazement he heard the unmistakable sound of Morse code traffic – 'did-dit, dit-dah-dit, dah-dit' etc.

'That's impossible!' Ray thought, 'a locked room, no-one in it, and the hand morse key functioning!'

Was it 'Henry' again? The Alkimos was totally without power, so how could anyone—or anything—possibly send morse messages?

Ray didn't investigate further. He'd had enough. He quickly got his tools and gear together, shut the door to the former Chief Steward's cabin, and carried everything out on to the open deck where he waited impatiently for his friend, Bob Hugill, to pick him up.

'How was it, Ray?' Hugill asked on the trip home. 'I'm looking forward to a good night's sleep in my own bed!' was Ray Krakouer's stoic reply.

Many others have stories to tell of their visits the Alkimos wreck.

Salvage workers cutting huge hunks of steel from her structure have reported eerie experiences.

An American exchange student became a temporary caretaker on board and left a diary of his creepy experiences: 'I was scared out of my wits!' he wrote.

A skeptical member of a TV crew felt an invisible 'someone' brush past them in a passageway, and recorded 'blood-curdling' screams and groans coming from an empty bunk during the night.

And others told more tales of dogs barking, drums rolling, cooking smells and heavy footsteps.

Finally, in July 1965, the Alkimos was officially declared a wreck. Yes, 'Henry' won! Did you doubt it for a single moment?

In the years following her eventual abandonment, many cray fishermen tending their pots claimed to have seen 'Henry' on board wearing an oilskin coat and possessing 'many ghost-like attributes.' Whatever that means!

Since then, large portions of the Alkimos' steel hulk have been cut, removed, ferried and sold as scrap. By 1998, practically nothing of the cursed lady protruded above sea level. Nature was the inevitable winner.

Or was 'Henry' the ultimate victor? The ship may be long gone, but 'Henry' remains alive in the annals of Australian maritime history as the 'Ghost Caretaker of the Alkimos'.

25. Bluestone Pub sells Spirits

'There's whistling upstairs, unexplained noises, stomping, glasses break, chairs and cutlery move...'

The heritage-listed, bluestone Coach and Horses Inn at Clarkefield – often described as 'Australia's most haunted hotel' – is twenty minutes drive from Melbourne's Tullamarine Airport.

Back in the gold rush days, it was the first Cobb & Co. staging post outside Melbourne on the way to the diggings at Mount Alexander and Bendigo – hence the extensive stable block at the rear (now used as an entertainment area for weddings and private functions).

At least two of the Coach and Horses' ghosts are associated with those rough and tumble days of gold-seekers, outlaws and ships' deserters. If you call into the Coach and Horses Inn these days the staff can provide a folder recording the hotel's history, including its hauntings, and other paranormal activities.

The commodious hotel was built by William Clarke in 1872 and comprises six ground floor rooms, including a bar, drawing room and parlor; plus seven upstairs bedrooms and a billiards room.

> Seeing that Mr Clarke is owner of all the land in the neighborhood of the [railway] station, we were wholly in his hands for whatever kind of accommodation he chooses to provide for us; consequently we have more reason to feel grateful at being provided for in such a superior manner. [Lancefield Courier, 31 October 1872]

When dead bodies were found in country towns during the era when the hotel was built, it was customary to place the corpse in the nearest hotel's cool room awaiting an inquest or removal to a more populous center. This may account for the high number of 'creepy' incidents at isolated country pubs.

The first such incident at the Coach and Horses involved a nameless Chinese miner returning from the goldfields. His body was found hanging from a rafter in the rear stables. His room had been ransacked and his personal possessions plundered.

It is easy to project that he'd been robbed of any gold he'd found; or that he disturbed a burglary in his room and was murdered to avoid identifying the intruder. Perhaps, when he found his precious gold missing and despaired at having to start all over again, he hanged himself. Maybe he was killed for his gold and strung up to make it appear like suicide.

Speculations about cause and effect are easy; but no further evidence is available of name, date, or circumstance—other than a lingering spirit which creates unease, chilly unexpected breezes and indistinct temporary sightings from upstairs windows.

Clarkefield, Victoria

There have been reported sightings of at least three ghostly presences with the most tragic being that of a ten-year-old autistic girl who was reputedly beaten to death by her father around the turn of the [previous] century. According to local folklore the girl witnessed a violent argument between her mother and father where the husband began to savagely beat his wife. The girl tried to intervene, and the father was so incensed that he beat her as well, leading to her death. Fearing retribution, he is supposed to have dumped her body into a well at the back of the hotel and then filled it in with dirt.

Later his wife left him and alerted authorities to the murder, but the girl's body was never recovered. It is said that she now haunts the upstairs part of the hotel, knocking on doors and crying. The father, who died soon after, most probably from suicide, is also said to haunt the building, and his presence is often felt in the ladies' toilet and the back dining room. [J G Montgomery, Haunted Australia: Ghosts of the Great South Land, Pennsylvania, 2016, p.210]

About a hundred years later (in 1983 to be precise), the old well behind the Coach and Horses Inn was in the news again:

A newspaper reporter spent a night alone in the stables behind the hotel in the hope of catching a ghost to write about. He didn't, but when walking past the infamous well the next morning he commented that the old pump mounted above the well was useless if it didn't work. The pump, he claimed, promptly came to life and started producing a steady stream of fresh water. When a plumber inspected it a few hours later the pump was found to be dry and completely seized up with rust. [Richard Davis, The Ghost Guide to Australia, (Bantam, 1998), p.203]

The owners at the time of the previous extraordinary incident were Don and Judy Busner, and when they decided to sell the business they though it incumbent on them to warn their successors that the place was haunted. The incoming owners, Frank and Sharon Nelson, were skeptical about ghosts – but the following tale demonstrates how quickly their beliefs changed!

Let's start with the story of Reagan's gold, and its repercussions:

Legend tells us of an Irish seaman named Patrick Reagan who

jumped ship in Melbourne and made his way to the goldfields where he 'struck it rich'.

Unfortunately, while stopping at the Clarkefield Hotel on his way back to Melbourne, Reagan was set upon by a group of dishonest police troopers who shot him [dead] and stole his gold. [Richard Davis, Great Australian Ghost Stories, Sydney, 2012, p.205]

In the early 1980s (perhaps a century after the initial incident), a medium from Penola, South Australia visited the hotel and reported sensing a gun battle between troopers and a lone stranger who tried to escape by running down the internal stairway. He didn't survive the attack.

Most people think the fugitive was Patrick Reagan.

An interesting parallel to this story happened when the new licensee, Frank Nelson, took over the Coach and Horses in March, 1984. He explained his experience to writer John Pinkney:

> I never had the faintest belief in ghosts till I moved into this place. But I had a fairly abrupt change of mind at about three o'clock on the morning of March 11.
>
> My wife Sharon and I were asleep upstairs, when we were wakened by noises in the front bar. We could hear people walking around – and bottles and glasses being rattled. Imagining we had intruders, I tiptoed to the top of the landing and started down.
>
> Suddenly, from the bottom of the stairway, I felt a blast of icy-cold air. Next, I was shoved in the back, with colossal force. I grabbed the banister, but the rail seemed to be gone. When I hit the deck, I turned to see who had pushed me.
>
> I couldn't believe it. There was no one there. The stairs were completely empty. [John Pinkney, A Paranormal File, Melbourne, 2000, p.19]

Frank couldn't see his attacker, and initially didn't feel any pain.

> When I went to get up, my foot was twisted back around. [He was immediately taken to hospital by ambulance]. They said it was impossible for me just to have fallen down stairs ... I would have to have fallen from a height – my ankle was shattered in three places, and I had to have three steel pins inserted. [Frank Nelson, 'Haunted' (TV documentary with Dr. Maurice Marsh). – Part 13, 1989]

Clarkefield, Victoria

Frank Nelson was on crutches for seven months. He had another truly frightening experience during his recovery period.

One night when he was in bed alone, he realized the bedroom door had opened and he felt the presence of something/somebody in the room. Next, he felt a hand grasp his plastered leg and start to twist it painfully. Frank grabbed his crutches lying beside the bed and thrashed around in the darkness to ward off his attacker. 'Get away! Get away!' he yelled.

By the time he limped to the door and put the light on, the door had already closed again – so this time Frank clicked the deadlock on, and went back to bed.

'Then the door opened again– that was it for me!' Frank said, 'I just lay there, going hot and cold. That incident convinced me there was some supernatural force at play!'

> News of the strange events occurring at the old hotel spread ...psychics, mediums, amateur ghost hunters and legions of thrill seekers converged on the hotel, demanding to be allowed to camp in the [Reagan] murder room and on the stairs.
>
> Eventually it became too much for the Nelsons and they departed. Their successors, Steve and Deborah Dudley, had an equally torrid time. They suffered every imaginable mishap. Equipment failed, including three washing machines in as many days. In a short time the Dudleys also departed in despair. [Richard Davis, The Ghost Guide to Australia, Bantam, 1998, p.204]

The Coach and Horses Inn changed hands yet again— this time the new owner employed another couple to run the business while he concentrated on restoring the grand old building to its original charm. As the new century approached, the hotel looked splendid with period-style décor and antique furnishings – and the owner/managers stayed around for a bit longer.

From 2005, Paul Levey and his partner Michele East ran the hotel for ten years – which the local newspaper, the Hume Leader, said made Paul 'the hotel's longest serving publican.'

Like Frank Nelson years before him, Paul Levey didn't

believe in ghosts when he started:

> I thought the stories were sort of not true ... but I have since changed my mind. There's whistling upstairs, unexplained noises, stomping upstairs, glasses break, chairs and cutlery move and you can come in the morning and the stove top is [switched] on.
>
> There's three types of people who come to the pub to see the ghosts. You have the people who come to take photos, you have the psychics and mediums, and then you have those dressed all in black who come on the full moon at midnight [Paul Levey, www.starweekly.com.au]

The hotel's next publican was Gus Holland who, fourteen months into the job, said he had yet to see a specter, but added that many 'ghost specialists' had visited the pub. 'They seem to think there's something around,' he said.

One subsequent 'ghost specialist' took his camera and recording equipment into the hotel and spent several hours seeking to identify and communicate with the resident ghosts. His 54-minute video can be seen by visiting the hotel's website.

Site details: https://www.clarkefieldcoachandhorsesinn.com/

26. The Ghost Who Rocks

...still jealously guarding her domain today

The penal museum at Port Arthur convict settlement attracts thousands of visitors annually.

However, not everyone you see there is necessarily a visitor. Some have been residing there for nearly two centuries!

Charles O'Hara Booth is one of them. A British military officer, Booth served in India and the West Indies before being appointed the first Commandant of the original settlement in 1833.

> Under his command the township of Port Arthur was laid out on an extensive scale, harbor construction carried out and reclamation undertaken, a government farm established at Safety Cove, and the semaphore telegraph system ... [Australian Dictionary of Biography, Vol.1, Melbourne University Press, 1966, F. C. Hooper]

Booth arranged for his own home to be erected on high ground on the fringe of the settlement, with a commanding view over the bay. It was a simple four-roomed timber cottage, with a separate kitchen linked to the house by a covered walkway.

Subsequent additions included gardens, stables and the high stone perimeter walls, all added by later

Commandants to create the imposing residence that remains today.

For five years, Booth lived alone in the house he designed until, in 1838, he married widow Elizabeth Eagle. His new bride and her two young children moved into the Commandant's house, and Booth engaged a nanny to help with his step-children's upbringing and to assist Elizabeth around the home.

Apparently, Nanny took her duties very seriously ...

> There's evidence Nanny's still jealously guarding her domain today. One day [recently] a visitor walked into a back room of the house and saw a woman sitting in a rocking chair. Brandishing a stick, she [Nanny] rudely ordered the woman to get herself and everybody else out! Nanny doesn't want anyone to stay very long, or mess things up. [Peter Richman Productions, Ghosts of Port Arthur, video documentary, 2003]

Either Nanny's spends a lot of time in her old rocking chair, or it seems the chair possesses a unique ability to self-activate!

> The old chair ... is very solid and only the strongest of gales is likely to make the chair move without human intervention. Yet on Christmas Eve in 1987, a Port Arthur employee found the chair rocking by itself.
>
> The employee, a non-believer in the paranormal, investigated every conceivable non-paranormal cause for the chair's freaky movements, including that strings were attached to the chair by a hoaxer, but no rational explanation was ever uncovered. [Tim the Yowie Man, Haunted & Mysterious Australia, New Holland, 2017, p.122]

There's another spooky aspect to Nanny's room at the back of the house:

> Attempts by visitors to take photographs inside the nanny's room sometimes produce quite unexpected results: cameras jam, flashes fail to work, and when someone does manage to take a photograph, faint shapeless blurs usually appear on the screen. [Richard Davis, Great Australian Ghost Stories, ABC Books, 2012, p.190]

Late one afternoon, when most of the visitors were getting ready to leave the settlement, some visitors witnessed a young child enter the Commandant's House through a side door—a door that had been locked by a guide after the last tour group left.

She was a fair-haired blue-eyed girl wearing a pinafore over a blue dress. No-one in authority had any idea who she was, or what she was doing there, or whether it was simply that the visitors had heard one too many ghost stories that day.

> There was another sighting the following day, and when this was researched, it was discovered there had been 10 sightings of this little girl over the years. One of the people who saw her thought her name started with a 'A' or an 'E', the other thought her name was 'Amy' or 'Emmy'.
>
> It is believed the little girl may be [the spirit of] Amelia Jane Booth, step-daughter of Charles O'Hara Booth who was Commandant in charge of the settlement from 1833. [Peter Richman Productions, Ghosts of Port Arthur, video documentary, 2003]

While it appears that Nanny and Amelia Jane linger at the Commandant's house, so too is the Commandant reluctant to leave! Charles O'Hara Booth has been observed several times by visitors, and is described as still wearing his full-dress uniform.

Booth had suffered a severe personal setback in 1838:

> He became lost in the bush of Forestier Peninsula with a convict assistant Joseph Turner. The pair lost their way in the central hills and became separated. Turner found his way to the house of a settler, Captain John Spotswood, who raised the alarm.
>
> Thomas Lempriere ... led the search party of soldiers, constables and settlers. By this time, Booth was three days overdue and had spend three nights in cold autumn weather, weak with hunger and with only his dogs for company.
>
> Finally, after another night, one of his dogs, Sandy, spotted a searcher and took him to Booth, who was frostbitten and too weak to call out. He was taken by boat and railway back to Port Arthur, but never fully recovered from the ordeal. [portarthur.org.au]

Following his brush with death, Commandant Booth experienced recurring bouts of a sudden fever which left him both physically and mentally overwhelmed. He retired from the army the following year and later moved his family to New Town, Hobart, where he died in 1851.

Perhaps he retained fond memories of the years he spent designing and commanding the settlement of Port Arthur, and had his physical and mental health not declined so rapidly, he would have continued to fulfill his duties there.

Among a group of recent visitors on a guided tour of the Commandant's House were a mother and her young daughter. During the visit, the child wandered off to other parts of the house. When her mother heard her little daughter chatting amiably with someone, she traced her daughter's voice to the Commandant's bedroom:

> She found her daughter beside the Commandant's bed, talking to an empty pillow. The mother held out her hand and said 'Come.'
>
> 'One moment, Mother,' the child responded. 'I'm having a nice talk with this man here, he's so sick.'

After telling the guide of this incident, they returned to the Commandant's bedroom where they found the perfect indentation of a man's body on the bedding.

☼

Site details: https://portarthur.org.au/visit/

27. Counting Monte Cristo's Ghosts

'a young male workman floating outside their bedroom window, staring in at them.'

When Reg Ryan purchased a rundown two-storey Georgian mansion in the NSW township of Junee in 1963 for a mere one-thousand pounds, he believed he'd bagged a bargain. Monte Cristo included servants' quarters, a chapel, stables, a ballroom and several acres of land.

Granted, it was rundown and in dire need of tender loving care, having been uninhabited for fifteen years. Or at least, so they thought.

During those years, the grand old house, with all its pretensions of splendor, had become a magnet for thieves, squatters and vandals. Windows were broken, doors had been removed, campfire ashes were piled up in various rooms and tree branches had grown through windows. Even the 'For Sale' sign had fallen down!

Two years earlier, the estate trustees had tried to ensure these acts of vandalism ceased by appointing Jack Simpson as caretaker. Alas, Simpson lasted only ten months before he was murdered by a local youth.

> After watching the movie 'Psycho' several times, the boy made his way up to the grounds of the homestead with a rifle and shot the

caretaker dead in his cottage. It is believed that he then scrawled the words 'die jack HA HA' on the wooden door, a macabre inscription that can still be seen to this day. [Alan Toner, Paranormal Australia, (ebook), 2014]

Undaunted by the amount of work required to turn the old mansion into a family home, Reg and his wife Olive and their three young daughters moved in and immediately got to work. Reg worked two jobs to make enough money to feed his family and educate his daughters while also acquiring materials for the re-building of his family's home.

In what he ironically described as his spare time, he renovated; restoring the sweeping gardens, reflooring the balcony and verandah, fitting cast-iron railings and installing opulent doors harvested from other mansions that had flowered and faded. [John Pinkney, Haunted: The Book of Australia's Ghosts, Melbourne, 2005, p.110]

It took only three days, though, for the Ryans to realize that all was not what it seemed at Monte Cristo.

Because there was neither power nor water, a relative was babysitting the children. After spending a day clearing rooms of rubble, the couple drove down to the town for supplies.

'It was very foggy that night,' Reg recalled. 'When we returned and came around the bottom corner of the driveway, light was streaming from every door and window...We sat there staring up at the house. It wasn't just lit, it was brilliantly lit – that's what we couldn't understand. There was no electricity connected!' [John Pinkney, Haunted: The Book of Australian Ghosts, Melbourne, 2005) p.108-9]

Reg turned the car's engine off, intending to walk up to the house to check what was going on. 'But the moment I pushed the car door shut,' Reg said, 'The lights went out – the house was in foggy darkness again.'

Olive also had an eerie experience with an unseen presence:

She felt a hand on her shoulder, she had heard her name being called, and heard footsteps on the balcony when no one was there, although she has never seen a ghost face to face – so to speak. [Darnley Sullivan, Ghosts of Australia, ebook, 2016]

The Ryans soon learned that they were sharing the house with a whole lot of different entities – and not all of them friendly. They had difficulties, too, with the children's pets. Cats, dogs and caged birds died mysteriously if kept inside the house. Outside dogs simply ran away.

What's it like bringing up a family in a haunted house?

'When the kids were younger it was just home and they accepted things,' Reg Ryan explains. '...it wasn't until they got a bit older they realized it wasn't normal. And of course by then they'd been living here all that time so it didn't worry them.' [Julie Miller & Grant Osborn, Something Is Out There, Sydney, 2010, p.24]

Author John Pinkney retells a Reg Ryan story about two of his daughters, Deborah and Noelene, who shared an upstairs bedroom during their childhood at Monte Cristo. Their room had a single large window at the side of the house, about 5 meters (about 17ft) above the ground. The girls would often complain to their parents that 'the man is back.' They would describe an apparition of the head and shoulders of a young male workman floating outside their bedroom window, staring in at them.

In 1977, when the girls' young brother Lawrence was five, their parents hosted a party in the ballroom and Lawrence was put to bed by one of his sisters. 'Every hour,' Lawrence recalls, 'one of the girls would pop their head into my room to check on me. My youngest sister, who was 12 at the time, entered my room to see a bearded man sitting on the end of my bed, staring at me. He then turned to give her a menacing stare. She screamed and ran to the party to tell my parents that there was a weird man in my room. When they got there, he was gone and I was sound asleep. They searched the house and found nothing or no one.'

Lawrence's sister described the man as wearing old-fashioned clothes.

Such regular paranormal incidents prompted Reg to thoroughly research the history of the property. What he found could have come straight from the pages of a 19th century novel.

The irony of calling the mansion Monte Cristo was not lost on Reg Ryan. Alexandre Dumas' 1844 book *The Count of Monte Cristo* was a torrid compelling story of romance, betrayal, selfishness and power.

So, too, was the history of the Ryan's family home!

By the time the railway line from Sydney to Melbourne was built through Junee in 1878, Christopher William Crawley had acquired over a thousand acres (400 hectares). He built a Railway Hotel (now Hotel Junee) and seven years later, flush with funds, built the grand two-storey Georgian mansion on a hill-top, providing expansive views of the district.

However, Crawley's estate echoed the misery of feudal times. Maids, servants and farm workers were drawn from the Junee township or lived on the property in harsh conditions, like peasants. Meanwhile, the 'ruling family' lived in their luxurious home overlooking their domain.

Mrs. Crawley ruled her household firmly. Her word was law, her judgments not to be queried. The seven Crowley children were all sent to boarding schools, and Monte Cristo became the center of the district's social life. Grand balls, garden parties, tennis and golf helped the local gentry while away their days.

However, under the surface of glitter and glamour, nothing was quite as it seemed.

Junee, N.S.W.

Intrigued to know more about the history of his family home, Reg Ryan conducted extensive research which today is contained in three thick scrapbooks. They contain details of violent deaths, many of which suggest that patriarch Christopher Crawley lead a double life – one as the wealthy squire, the other as a sinister, sexual predator.

> ... a young servant girl, who, upon finding herself pregnant to her employer, flung herself to her death from the mansion's first floor balcony. [Miller & Osborn, Something Is Out There, Sydney, 2010, p.6]

She struck the ground on the concrete steps leading to Monte Cristo's front door immediately under the edge of the balcony, and died instantly. There, on the top step, one can still see a strange contrasting pale area which, we're told, was caused by the bleach they used to clean up the blood which had soaked into the concrete!

This event took on even more gruesome overtones when Reg Ryan met an elderly lady who had worked as a day maid in the Crawley home at the time of this incident. She swore to Reg that she saw Christopher Crawley push the poor girl off the balcony to her death. 'Then it was all hushed up,' she added.

Another mind-bending tale came to light during Reg Ryan's investigations. Mrs. Crawley's sister, Mrs. Steele, worked at Monte Cristo as a live-in housekeeper, and for reasons that will become obvious in the next quote, stayed on after her employers' eventual deaths.

> She ... had an illegitimate child to Crawley, called Harold. He was developmentally disabled, and he was chained up in a [rear] shed. After both Mr. and Mrs. Crawley had passed away, Mrs. Steele stayed on with the boy.
>
> When she didn't show up in town for supplies after a few days, authorities investigated. They found both mother and child on the brink of death. She was taken to the local hospital, but died on the way ... [Harold] fretted to death because he knew no other life than being chained in a back shed. [Julie Miller & Grant Osborn, Something is Out There, (Sydney, 2010), pps .8,9]

Research also shed some light on Crawley's sadistic nature.

Many years ago... a young man named Morris worked at Monte Cristo and slept in the stables. One day he complained of being too ill to work, but his boss thought he was shirking and rashly put a match to the straw mattress the boy lay on. Morris was genuinely ill and unable to get up. He burned to death. [Richard Davis, Great Australian Ghost Stories, Sydney, 2012, p.277]

Ralph Morris' death was investigated by the local police, we are told, but because his boss (Mr. Crawley) 'probably didn't mean to kill him,' no charges were laid.

> Christopher William Crawley died at Monte Carlo in 1910 after a carbuncle on his neck (caused by the high, starched collars he wore) became infected. His widow, Elizabeth, lived on in the great house for another twenty-three years, leaving it on only two occasions. [Richard Davis, Great Australian Ghost Stories, Sydney, 2012, p.273]

So, who haunts Monte Cristo?

There does not appear to be any references to ghostly visitors prior to William Crawley's death in 1910. Ah, but in 1911 – just a year after his passing – an infant died in unusual circumstances:

> ...the death of Crawley's baby daughter who slipped from her nanny's arms and down the stairs, subsequently dying from her injuries ... the maid claimed that something pushed the baby from her grasp. [J. G. Montgomery, Haunted Australia – Ghosts of the Great Southern Land, Pennsylvania, 2016, p.42]

Even today, this stairwell is markedly cold, and many young visitors feel extremely anxious when climbing the stairs here. Many adults record feeling 'invisible hands' touching them—sometimes even pressing down quite hard against them—while on these stairs.

One recorded account of this was when a mother and daughter – both visitors – got 'stuck' on the stairs, being unable to either go up or down because they felt an 'invisible force' keeping them there. They were ultimately able to proceed with their tour when several other visitors joined them and they moved forward en masse.

The Ryan's themselves continued to experience strange

Junee, N.S.W.

presences.

> Olive [Mrs Ryan] believes that the ghosts of the Crawleys, particularly Mrs. Crawley, follow her around: 'all day, every day. I often hear a phantom playing the piano and even someone calling my name. I'm sure they do it just to make us feel we are intruders in their house.'
>
> When I hang things on the walls, they will often fall down until I relocate them to where Mrs. Crarley approves of them,' adds Olive, who has learnt to live with and accept nightly ghostly goings-on. [Tim the Yowie Man, Haunted and Mysterious Australia, Sydney, 2017, pps36-37]

The sounds of the piano playing are interesting. There hasn't been a piano at Monte Cristo since 1948!

Reg and Olive Ryan held the first Monte Cristo Charity Ball in 1973, and it has since become an annual event raising almost a million dollars for charity. In 1992, Mrs. Ryan's nephew Neil and his girlfriend attended the ball, which ended in the early hours of the morning. When his girlfriend wanted to use the bathroom before retiring, she felt uneasy and asked Neil to escort her and wait outside the bathroom door. Which he did.

> After waiting in the hallway for her, Neil proceeded to escort her back towards the stairs which lead to their room; suddenly from the top of the darkened stairs, a voice seemed to drift from nowhere, looking up they both saw a young woman dressed in white who said softly twice: 'Don't worry, it will be all right' and vanished before their eyes. [abovetopsecret.com]

In 1990 – almost three decades after the Ryans purchased Monte Cristo – their 21-year old son Lawrence drove home from a social outing in Wagga Wagga. As he turned into the driveway, he saw Monte Cristo emanating a brilliant light through every window, just as his parents had in 1963. And as they had all those years ago when the Ryan's were the new owners of the house, the lights all turned off abruptly as he drove closer!

Reg Ryan's scrapbook includes numerous paranormal experiences reported by visitors to the mansion, as well as some blurred photographs and spine-chilling reports by ghost-hunters, mediums and psychics.

GHOSTS DOWN UNDER

Regular 'Ghost Tours' are conducted, with accommodation and meals available if booked ahead. Included in the tour are Reg's outstanding collection of rejuvenated horse-drawn carriages kept in the stable block.

After more than half a century in residence at Monte Cristo, Reg Ryan passed over. In their issue dated 7 July 2014, the Wagga Daily Advertiser announced:

> One of Junee's most well-known residents, Reg Ryan, died on Sunday. Mr. Ryan was the owner, along with his wife Olive, of the historic Monte Cristo homestead, widely regarded as the most haunted house in Australia.

Then, a few weeks later, yet another surprise ...

> A month after Monte Cristo owner Reg Ryan died, it is believed he has returned to the homestead – joining the other spirits still residing in the house ... Mr. Lawrence Ryan said a recent tour guest sent a photo which he believes is his father's spirit returning to the house he restored from a wreck and developed into a thriving business. [Junee Southern Cross, 20 August, 2014]

The photograph, taken in the stables with the restored horse-drawn carriages, shows a blurred image of a 'person' among the vehicles. No doubt it will join the dozens of other pieces of evidence in the thick scrapbooks for visitors to inspect.

As the Wagga Daily Advertiser wrote:

> ...the historic Monte Cristo homestead [is] ... widely regarded as the most haunted house in Australia.

☼

Site details: https://www.montecristo.com.au/

28. A Ghost on the Bridge

*'We all stood looking at each other
in mute fear and astonishment'*

When Thomas Scott visited Pinjarrah, fifty miles south of Perth, for four days during the early 1870s, he saw an elderly lady standing on the bridge over the local river, the Murray.

Later, he mentioned the incident to an associate, and the 'ghost on the bridge' story quickly re-surfaced around the town. The locals knew whose ghost it was! She had even visited the very hotel Scott was staying at, The Exchange, and walked along its passageways knocking on doors in a truly ghostly manner!

Thomas Scott wrote about his sighting, and what he learned about 'The Ghost on the Old Bridge,' in his oddly-named book 'Travels among Gold and Cannibals in Western Australia, 1870-1874,' telling of his trip from Albany, overland to Perth, and eventually to Northampton, a distance of 540miles/870kms. The National Library of Australia describes Thomas Scott's book as an 'idiosyncratic travelogue.'

Scott had told 'Mr C.' [probably Mr Cornish] what he saw:

GHOSTS DOWN UNDER

It was only last night, rather late, that I came across the old bridge and met none save one solitary individual, an elderly lady to all appearances, who was attired in a light, loose dress. [Thomas Scott, Travels among Gold and Cannibals in Western Australia, 1870-1874, Perth, W.A.]

To which his companion replied:

My poor Aunt, Mrs C., who has been dead for the past seven years, and this is the anniversary of her mysterious death. Why, this is the veritable ghost of the old bridge of which I was just speaking to you about, and which makes its nocturnal appearance on the old bridge every year around this time.

Whether it is the disembodied spirit of my Aunt, which carries her features and is recognized by all of us, or whether it is but a phantom of the mind, God only knows, for it is very mysterious. [T. Scott, Travels... in Western Australia, Perth, W.A.]

Thomas Scott then suggested Mr C. was 'laboring under some illusion,' and inquired 'in what manner she met her death?'

No illusion whatever – it is too true. She walks the bridge towards midnight nine days in each year just before and after the anniversary of her death. She has been recognized by her two sisters, her brother John, and Mr Koil, my uncle.

She was found dead seven years ago on the old bridge. She was supposed to have died from an apoplectic fit, but whatever the cause of death was she was interred next day as the weather was too oppressive to keep her any longer than that short time. [Mr C., in T. Scott, Travels... in Western Australia, Perth, W.A.]

Drawing a deep breath, Mr C. then revealed some fascinating details of the ghost's visits to the bridge, and their home:

On the 1st July, one year from the date of her demise, she, or rather her apparition... was first seen by my Uncle at midnight walking the old bridge like a silent sentinel from the place of departed spirits.

My Uncle came home – I remember the night well – just as he had finished telling us what he had seen, three distinct, loud knocks were heard at our back door. It was a beautiful moonlit starry night – not a cloud was seen in the vast blue firmament; and bewildering stillness seemed to reign supreme. There was no time for anybody

Pinjarrah, West Australia

to have made off nor was there any place of concealment near at hand, as instantaneously we all ran to the door – but there was nothing to be seen and there was not a breath of air stirring. With palpitating hearts and big drops of perspiration on our foreheads we returned to the house.

The door was hardly closed when three more knocks, louder than the first, was again heard and at the same time as distinctly as possible my uncle's Christian name repeated two or three times outside the door. The sound or voice was that of my Aunt, which was recognized by all present. We all stood looking at each other in mute fear and astonishment – terror seemed to sway every heart now beating three times as fast.

My Uncle was the first to break the spell. He rushed to the door, closely followed by myself, as if ashamed of his momentary fear, to behold a tall, stately figure of a female clad in a light loose dress similar to that she had on at the time she was found dead on the old bridge.

State Library of Western Australia

But that was not all that happened that evening. Mr C's Uncle knew it was his deceased sister, Kate, or her apparition. He continued:

> She was walking or rather slowly gliding, as it were, in the direction of the old bridge, which is about a quarter of a mile/·4km from our farm.

My Uncle instinctively shouted 'Kate,' his sister's name. But, as if by magic, on her name being called, she immediately disappeared from our view.

We all proceeded to the old bridge with the expectation of seeing the apparition there, for we were all fully convinced now that the figure was nothing else, but we were disappointed. None of us slept that night, but kept a vigil till morning.

Three nights after this appearance, the ghost returned once more – but disappeared as soon as it was approached.

After that it made a series of re-appearances on the days surrounding the anniversary of Aunt Kate's death. 'Each succeeding year to the present one,' Mr C. told Thomas Scott, 'has brought us the ghostly visits of my deceased Aunt.'

Having completed this 'background briefing' for his visitor, Mr C. reminded Thomas Scott that the anniversary of his Aunt's death had almost completed another calendar year, and that a family group would be waiting that very evening at the bridge to welcome the apparition again.

'You are welcome to join our little private party, if you wish,' Mr C. said.

'I shall be too glad to accept your offer,' I replied, 'and I only hope I shall have a glimpse of your nocturnal visitant. May I bring a friend?' 'Certainly, with pleasure – half a dozen if you like – the more the merrier.' [T. Scott, Travels... in Western Australia, Perth, W.A.]

Scott informed a friend, nominated as 'Mr M', of his midnight venture and its purpose, and Mr M readily agreed to accompany him.

At midnight on that day they all proceeded to the bridge. Half the group stationed themselves at one end and the rest on the opposite end.

They waited for nearly an hour and then all saw the apparition walking half way along the bridge. At a pre-arranged signal they all converged on the spot where the ghost stood but by that time there was nothing there. Whatever it was had completely vanished into thin air. Everyone in that party was perfectly sane and sober.
[Miriam Howard-Wright, Eyewitness, Australian Ghosts, Artlook, W.A., p. 169]

Pinjarrah, West Australia

On the next anniversary of Aunt Kate's death – a year after Thomas Scott had seen the apparition for himself – a group of local lads lay in wait for her appearance, intent on capturing her/it. Aunt Kate simply didn't show up, and she was never seen again.

29. 'I'm Related to Your Ghost'

'showing her the sympathy she never received in life.'

'Ascot House,' has seen many owners and occupiers since it began life as Toowoomba's largest and most elaborate 'grand residence' in 1876.

One occupant, however, remained there for over a hundred and thirty years.

The house was first constructed as a private resident for successful Toowoomba storekeeper Frederick Holberton. It was designed and built in an unusual U-shape, with verandahs reaching beyond the length of the house. It was set on land extending on its western side close to the local racecourse.

Holberton named his home 'Tor'. Within its extensive grounds, it had stables, tennis courts, croquet greens, fishponds, and walking paths through imported trees and shrubbery.

A large staff was required to help run the establishment, so Holberton engaged grooms, coachmen, gardeners, cooks and domestic maids. One of the maids, a local lass named Maggie Hume – who returns to our story later – began employment at 'Tor' when she was a mere twelve years old.

Toowoomba, Queensland

In 1899, Holberton moved on, selling 'Tor' to the flamboyant and rich William Beit, who re-named it Ascot. Thirteen years later it was on the market again, but when it failed to find a purchaser, Beit sold off the parklands and left the grand mansion standing on just two acres.

Over the next sixty years 'Ascot House passed through several hands. It is said the U.S. Army billeted troops there during World War Two. Later in the 1940s, the then owner added nine small flats to the existing house, but cheap accommodation attracted the wrong sort of tenants and maintenance was neglected. Windows were broken, vandalism was rife, and the gardens were left untended.

Then, in 1984, two visitors arrived at 'Ascot House.'

Miss Lois Jackman and a friend paid a visit on her friend's brother, who was renting 'one of the nine scruffy, barely livable flats.'

> 'There was rubbish everywhere – and when my friend, holding a candle, took me up into the gothic tower, we almost lost our footing on the rubble and broken plaster littering the stairs.'

> Ascot was a mess. But that afternoon, seemingly against all reason, Lois made a firm decision. She would become the owner of this house – no matter what obstacles might confront her. [John Pinkney, Haunted: the Book of Australia's Ghosts, Melbourne, 2005, pps. 13-14]

Within days, Miss Lois Jackman had signed the Bill of Sale for 'Ascot House.' A few weeks later she moved in, fully aware the sad old house would required a major renovation but determined to bring it back to its former glory.

> Almost every physical element of the mansion, from roofs and gutters to floors and plumbing, was on the edge of ruin. The flats, with their population of drifters, had been slums for generations.
> [John Pinkney, Haunted, p.14]

Lois Jackman discovered the unused upper storey had several smashed windows leaving it exposed to the weather; making it a favored retreat for nesting birds. Lois later recalled that: '103 garbage bags of pigeon droppings, nests and dead birds were removed from upstairs.'

Ascot House could have been used as a setting for a ghostly movie, but the skills of Hollywood were not needed for things to go bump in the night in this decrepit old mansion.

Soon after the renovation got underway, Lois Jackman had several slightly unnerving experiences.

Late one night she heard footsteps in the corridor passing her bedroom. Noiselessly making her way to the bedroom door, she flung it open, expecting to confront the intruder. The passage was empty. She nervously returned to her bed, but sat and listened intently, convinced someone—or something—was moving around her home in the small hours of the darkest night.

There was another thing, too. Nothing to really worry about but, on a couple of occasions, Miss Jackman noticed that chairs had been moved around overnight. They weren't shifted to another room, just re-positioned. It always happened when no-one else was in the house.

One day, an elderly neighbor who had lived in Newmarket Street for more than 70 years, called in to see how the renovations were shaping up. The neighbor reminisced about playing with the children from 'Ascot' as a young girl.

Then she mentioned that her young friends had told her of a ghost they had occasionally seen there. She wondered if Lois might have seen it too.

Lois Jackman truthfully replied that she hadn't, but the conversation planted a seed in Lois's mind.

Maybe, just maybe, she thought, something paranormal was going on in 'Ascot House.'

> 'Shortly after my chat with that neighbor, I had a quite unsettling experience... It was about 2 a.m. and I was walking across a large empty room...when I was about halfway, I got a shock.
>
> Someone dragged their finger across my left shoulder. I swung around to confront whoever it was. No one was there...
>
> 'A few minutes later I had to go back across that room... I was jumpy and quite scared. And reasonably so, as it turned out, because at about the same spot as before, the finger made its dragging movement again ...this time across the right shoulder. I didn't bother turning around – I just got out of there.' [Miss Lois Jackman in John Pinkney's Haunted: The Book of Australia's Ghosts, p.16]

After that incident, Lois Jackman began asking other long-term neighbors about their knowledge of ghosts at 'Ascot House.' One person she checked with was the 'brother of a friend' who had brought her to 'Ascot House' on her first visit.

He confessed that he had actually seen the ghost of a young woman slumped against a wall in one of the rooms!

Others she spoke to recalled stories of a broken-hearted girl who was killed or died 'early last century'. Someone else told of a servant who had committed suicide back in 'Ascot's' halcyon days, soon after the Folly was built.

But there were no names and no dates. There was nothing she could check or verify.

While all this 'spooky' stuff was very interesting to Miss Jackman, she still had renovations to complete and an income to earn. She had invested large amounts of energy and money towards bringing 'Ascot House' back to its pristine glory and had no time to indulge in macabre tales of restless spirits.

In 1992, the restoration of 'Ascot House' was complete. Lois Jackman took pride in her work, and in October that year the property was added to the Queensland Heritage

Register. Two years later, the premises were opened to the public as 'Ascot House Tea Rooms and Museum'.

With all her hard work behind her, Miss Jackman had time to consider the ghostly stories she had been told. Sometimes, while serving tea and scones in the Tea Rooms or showing guests through the museum, she told them about her neighbors' recollections of a ghostly presence in the house. Sometimes, she even mentioned her own eerie experiences, adding that she would love to know who it was who walked the halls at night.

Word of her quest spread far and wide. Then, in 2004, Lois Jackman received an unexpected telephone call.

'I'm related to your ghost,' the female caller said, 'Your ghost was my grandmother's stepsister!'

A meeting between the pair was arranged, and Lois learned that her caller had stumbled upon an account of the 'Ascot House' ghost while preparing her family tree.

It transpired that 12-year-old Maggie Hume began work in 1880 as a maid at Tor—as it was then known. In 1891, aged just 23, she died on the premises.

At first, Lois Jackman was uncertain she had found her ghost. She was aware that 'Dying on the premises' did not mean the young girl was destined to walk the passageways of Tor for eternity, but further surprises were soon revealed.

Lois Jackman read her informant's scrapbook of supporting information.

She learnt that Mr Holberton was absent on the fateful morning, and the staff— aware that Maggie had not arrived for breakfast—knocked loudly on her door. There was no response. The gardener placed a ladder against her exterior wall and saw Maggie lying absolutely still in bed, attired in her nightdress. They summoned the police.

Her body was found on her small bed in the servant's quarters by Constable McKenna and the coachman Joseph Davis.

As Miss Jackman browsed through the scrapbook, she found police records, newspaper articles, and even more telling, the autopsy report, which stated that Maggie's death had been caused by her taking four grains of strychnine poison.

> According to police at the time, Maggie Hume had suicided after learning she was pregnant.

> Two male staff members confessed that they had had what they called 'connection' with her. [John Pinkney, Haunted: The Book of Australia's Ghosts, p.19]

The Constable searched Maggie's room and found three letters addressed to Maggie's aunt, a resident of Toowoomba, bequeathing her certain small amounts of money and 'a bag of lemons behind the door'.

> Official police records show that there was an urgency to get rid of her body.

> Maggie was found dead in her bed in the morning (24-7-1891), a post-mortem was conducted at the hospital morgue that same day and she was buried on the following day in an unmarked grave. [Don Talbot, Ghostly Tales of Toowoomba, p.7]

Having established the most-likely identity of 'Ascot House's ghost, Miss Jackman took a further, unusual step:

> 'Because she was a single woman who killed herself she was buried in an unmarked grave. A caretaker at Drayton Cemetery has shown us where her plot is, so we'll know exactly where to put a plaque. It will be our way of showing her the sympathy she never received in life.' [Miss Lois Jackman, in Pinkney's Haunted: The book of Australia's Ghosts, p. 20]

Will this charitable action finally give Maggie Hume's restless soul the peace she so desperately seeks? Perhaps. But if not, at least Lois Jackman will no longer feel the need to sit up all night in terror, listening for approaching footsteps of a tormented spirit.

☼

[Privately owned]

30. Violence From Beyond

'spirit figures still roam the deserted corridors

Aradale, the 'largest abandoned mental institution in Australia,' sits majestically on a hill overlooking the township of Ararat on the Western Highway, just over 200kms / 125miles from Melbourne.

Visitors, even 'sticky beaks,' were made welcome during the asylum's early days. Seven years after it opened in 1867, the Geelong Advertiser carried this story:

> As for going through the place, the only formality to be observed is an application to the attendant, who, after entering your name in a large book, shows you over the establishment. At present the number of male patients is 210, and there are 160 females confined as patients ...

> The first ward visited was the idiot ward, and truly no more melancholy sight could be imagined ...than the unfortunates who are consigned for the rest of their lives to that place ... [Geelong Advertiser, 25 June 1874, p. 3]

Someone who wasn't 'consigned for the rest of their life' at Aradale was 'Old Margaret.'

> Perhaps the most disturbing rumor of all ... is that of 'Old Margaret'. The legend goes that 'Old Margaret' was detained in the asylum at a very early age but was kicked out when the entire facility was closed in 1998.

[Since her subsequent death] they say 'Old Margaret' regularly returns, tracing the halls of a now abandoned asylum that it is the only place she ever called home. [Dominic Cansdale, Moustache Magazine (online), 23 October 2014]

Aradale

Peter Duncan was a Maintenance employee while Aradale was operating and stayed on as Caretaker of the 63-building complex when it was vacated by both hospital staff and patients in 1998. For many years he was the only one around. Well, the only living presence, at least. Whenever he heard the sound of footsteps or doors closing in the empty buildings, he knew 'Old Margaret' was paying a visit. 'She never caused any trouble,' Peter says, smiling.

Nurse Kerry was in charge of the women's ward and no doubt took good care of Old Margaret. Perhaps she is still keeping her safe.

It is said the good nurse liked her patients ('the inmates') but not the visitors. They were disruptive. They asked too many questions and they invariably stayed too long. Her dislike of prying visitors appears to have intensified after her death and since Aradale ceased operation.

The most frequently seen spirit is Nurse Kerry. People see her wandering around in her nurse's uniform ... she seems to keep the spirits calm as she did when they were alive, and she watches over people [visitors] as they comes through. [Bill Tabone, Australian Paranormal Society, Haunting Australia TV series, 2015]

Nurse Kerry often scares ghost tour visitors in the women's wing. Some report unexplained pains, others say they had their hair pulled, were physically touched or shoved by someone, probably her.

The late Indian metaphysicist, Rev. Gaurav Tiwari may have captured Nurse Kerry's image on his full-spectrum camera, which reads both ultra-violet and infra-red, as well as white light. On his photograph, a woman wearing a nurse's uniform can be seen at a distance as a full-bodied apparition.

> I heard footsteps coming towards me. I could see nothing on the screen of my camera. I started taking pictures. One picture shows a shadow figure at the far end of the corridor. [Gaurav Tiwari, Haunting Australia, Episode 3, 2015]

His night-time photograph provided evidence that spirit figures still roam the deserted wards and corridors of Aradale. The captured fleeting image appears in a single frame. Most viewers say it was Nurse Kerry's ghost still keeping her eye on pesky visitors.

Today's female wards don't have an aggressive ambience. 'As a matter of fact,' says Bill Tabone of Australian Paranormal Society, ' It's quite playful at times.'

> The female [spirits], I think, appreciate people being there, they enjoy it. The ward is quite active, and not aggressive. One weekend we were there and actually captured 87 Class A EVPs [Electronic Voice Phenomena]—as clear as you and I speaking. You are dealing with intelligent spirits there. [Bill Tabone on Parasearch UK Radio, with Penny Morgan, 1 November 2017]

Eighty-seven clear, recorded messages is an outstanding weekend's achievement by both sides of the veil!.

The male wards, however, are a different story. According to Bill Tabone:

> One weekend we were on the bottom floor of the men's ward. There is something quite nasty down there, and it doesn't like me very much! I came out and had three big scratches straight down the back of my head, that's not unusual but I was scratched really badly. [Bill Tabone on Parasearch UK Radio, with Penny Morgan, 1 November 2017]

Tabone also described one unusual encounter involving a doppelganger (where a 'look-alike' or double of a living person is involved). In this instance the doppelganger was Bill Tabone's wife, Amanda, a fellow paranormal researcher:

> We were outside having a break, and Lionel [another researcher with them] was having a cigarette [around the corner].
>
> Lionel saw Amanda sticking her head around a corner of the men's ward calling 'Lionel, we need you! Lionel, we need you! Bill's hurt!' with the voice coming from inside the building.
>
> Luckily Lionel knew where we [Bill & Amanda] were, and came around the building to us and told me what had happened.
>
> There was a nasty, little energy in there, I believe, trying to lure Lionel into this building on his own.

Bill and Lionel then entered the men's ward together for another quick look around. There was no-one there:

> When we decided to leave, we closed the outside door behind us, and sat down on a railing ... and within thirty seconds there was something behind that closed door, pounding it hard, trying to come out! [Bill Tabone on Parasearch UK Radio, with Penny Morgan, 1 November 2017]

The mens' wards may be aggressive, even weird, but in a separate building, under Aradale's jurisdiction, stood the notorious 'J Ward' where 'aggression' truly reigned.

When the local Ararat jail was closed, 'J Ward' became the secure jail holding Victoria's most difficult prisoners, those who were criminally insane – psychopaths, murderers, deviates and belligerents.

The nature of some of 'J Ward's inmates was revealed at a meeting of the Lunacy Commission held in August 1885 and reported in Melbourne's Advocate newspaper. An ex-warder at Ararat, E.J. Saunders, gave the following evidence:

> To my knowledge, three men who have committed murder at different times are still in the same yard with other inmates of the asylum. Two of them killed fellow patients in the asylum, one with an axe and the other with a billet of wood taken from a shed. [Advocate, 22 August 1885, p.11]

Little wonder the unseen entities still residing in 'J Ward' today have a reputation for shoving, scratching and even yelling at tourists invading their space.

> Until it closed a hundred years later, some of the most depraved and notorious criminals in Australia lived and died there ...many of the inmates refuse to leave [after death] and linger on to terrify those who dare to enter their territory.
>
> J Ward holds a number of dubious records. Incarcerated within its walls were both the youngest and oldest criminals in Australian history. Boys as young as 12 were sent to endure horrific conditions J Ward had to offer, while the unfortunate Bill Walker lived to the ripe age of 108, serving a true life sentence for his crimes. [realparanormalexperiences.com/Ararat-lunatic-asylum-the-haunting]

Walker spent 60 years in J Ward. His crime? He was an early anti-smoking advocate who asked a man smoking a cigarette in a café to butt it out. The smoker refused, so Bill Walker drew his gun and shot him in the head. He was found to be insane and was carted off to 'J Ward'. There was no trial, no jury. Two medical signatures was all it took.

Maybe that's just as well. Bill Tabone tells a story of Walker as a little old man who—when someone tried to take a piece of food off his plate – stabbed them with his fork! His aggressive tendencies seemed not to have abated with age!

Another unruly prisoner was Gary Webb, a very disturbed individual who self-mutilated in his cell on seventy occasions. His spirit, too, is angry and aggressive, and EVP (Electronic Voice Phenomena) recorders used by paranormal investigators have caught him yelling 'Get Out!' at their intrusion.

Bill Tabone had a brief encounter with a male at J. Ward. Here's his account:

> Just outside the compound itself there's a forensic building, and we take visitors there. I had a lady with me when I opened the front door of this building; there was a short, stout man standing [inside] there dressed in an old woolen [prison] uniform that they used to wear.

Ararat, Victoria

He looked at us for two or three seconds, he was as confused as we were, and then he vanished.

I looked at this lady and she said, 'Did you see that?'

I said 'Yep!' We get things like that all the time. [Bill Tabone on Parasearch UK Radio, with Penny Morgan, 1 November 2017]

'J Ward' was closed in 1991, and is now a museum.

It's well worth a visit …. if you dare!

☼

Site details: https://www.jward.org.au/ghost-tours/

31. A Hitch-Hiking Ghost

'He said he didn't lose his mind'

After a sometimes hair-raising drive along a road clinging to the steeply-sided ridges of a spur of the Great Dividing Range, intrepid travellers to Jenolan Caves are rewarded with a view of the bitumen road surface disappearing into the black, gaping maw of the twenty-four-meter high Grand Arch. The spectacular introduction to Jenolan Caves is matched by what is on offer underground ... [Illustrated Guide to Australian Places, Sydney, 1995, p. 88]

Jenolan Caves, Australia's best-known limestone cave system, is 175 kms [108 miles] west of Sydney.

The caves are exciting, extensive, and mysterious. So are their ghosts!

One current Cave Guide tells of being tapped on the shoulder several times by 'no-body' (literally), having her leg grabbed and shaken by an unseen force on the stairs, and of seeing orbs briefly in the Mud Tunnel.

Another Guide —one who tended to be a skeptic about such occurrences—was in the 'Shrine' area of the 'Ribbon Cave'- at the very dead-end of the passage when he heard footsteps approaching from behind.

As he was doing maintenance work and not conducting a tour, no-one else should have been there. Yet the footsteps continued. They stopped right behind him. Then he heard a sound like a person clearing their throat. Wow!

So much for his skepticism. He took off, running from the cave as fast as he could, not looking back for a split second.

Once outside, he realized he'd broken a cardinal rule by leaving the lights on. A conscientious guide, he timidly returned to the cave to switch them off, carefully checking to ensure there was no one else lurking.

Did he believe a ghost had been standing behind him? 'Well, I didn't.' he said later,' but I can't explain it any other way!'

At another time, the same guide was walking through the Lucas Cave collecting litter. He paused for a while in the 'Cathedral' and became aware of a dark figure on the other side of the chamber. When he shone his torch at the figure, the light from the torch mysteriously died. Turning the torch away from the figure made it work again.

He began to suspect the figure was more ghostly than human.

As he progressed through the cave, the figure followed from a distance.

Each time he shone his torch in the direction of the figure, the light died; yet as soon as he faced it in the opposite direction, it came back on again.

This happened throughout the cave. With considerable difficulty, the skeptical guide eventually had no choice but accept that the figure was one of Jenolan's ghosts who was apparently keeping an eye on him!

That's hardly surprising, considering that many of the Jenolan guides insist that two old tour guides, long since deceased, still loiter around Jenolan caves and appear to have made their spiritual home in these familiar surroundings.

While their re-appearance sometimes startles visitors, to most of the living tour guides, they're simply friendly supervisors.

One of these may very well be James Wiburd.

Known to his friends as 'Voss', James was a veteran caver. He was employed as a guide at Jenolan in 1885 at the age of 18, and in 1903 he became Superintendent, a position he retained until his retirement in 1932 at the age of 65.

Throughout those years, James Wiburd regularly explored the numerous labyrinthine extensions with only the flickering light of a candle to guide him. Several exciting caves he discovered have since been opened up to visitors.

> James Wiburd died in 1942. 'It is said that ... [his] ashes were buried at Jenolan 'in an inaccessible crevice deep in the labyrinth to which he devoted his life'. [www.jenolancaves.org.au/blog/ghost-or-geological-phenomenon/, 2015]

The Jenolan Caves were his life, so one can understand why such familiar and beloved surroundings would become James Wiburd's spiritual home. Perhaps as a long-term superintendent, he also feels the need to continue supervising the new guides.

Here's a story told to us by one of the Cave Guides:

> Sometimes we have wedding ceremonies conducted in 'The Cathedral' at Jenolan Caves. This particular bride later returned to become one of our Tour Guides.

Jenolan Caves, N.S.W.

A guest at her wedding was her Great Aunt, a 'sensitive' who could perceive the 'other world'.

'Who is that strange man standing behind the best man?' asked Great-Aunt. 'He looks very stern and serious.'

When told there wasn't anyone standing behind the best man, she replied 'I can never tell the difference between the living and the passed on.'

She was then asked to describe the man and his clothing. It was a perfect description of James Wiburd, identified from photographs in our collection. [Cory Camilleri, Jenolan Guide in Live 90.5 Radio interview, 2014]

Another experience is told on the Jenolan Caves website. Again, the finger of suspicion is pointed at explorer, guide and caretaker James Wiburd.

Here is an abbreviated version of Cave Guide Geoff Melbourne's account:

> I was taking a regular tour through the River Cave. The path runs alongside the Pool of Reflections and I leant over the railing looking into the crystal clear water and saw something on the bottom.
>
> Someone standing next to me said, 'It's a button off an old tunic. Look, there's another one over there.' I didn't look at the person speaking, and after staring into the water a few moments more, I started moving the group on; but there was no-one standing next to me!
>
> The closest man was several meters away, and he called out, 'What happened to the guy in between us?' I asked him what he looked like, and was told 'He was a tall man wearing a rumpled gray suit.' There was nobody of that description in the group.
>
> I then asked the group if any of them had spoken to me about the button in the water. They all shook their heads, no-one knew what I was talking about!

But this anecdote isn't quite finished yet ...

A week later the same guide passed the spot again with another group. One visitor said he was glad to get out of that part of the River Cave.

'Why?' the guide asked.

'I saw someone in the shadows sitting on a rock watching us,' he was told.

'What did he look like?' queried the guide.

'Oh, he was an old man in a suit!' came the reply.

The guide speculates the person who spoke to him (and the one seen in the shadows on a rock a week later) was the spirit of James Wiburd. [www.jenolancaves.org.au/blog, 2015]

The other former Guide frequently seen in and around Jenolan Caves is the first-ever Guide, Jeremiah Wilson, who was appointed 'Keeper' in 1867- almost two decades before James Wiburd was employed as a Guide.

Many believe that Jeremiah Wilson still remains at Jenolan Caves today, along with his wife, Lucinda.

Tour Guide Cory Camilleri recalled a story involving Jeremiah:

> I was conducting one of our tours and passing through a section that is relatively spooky – with rustic handrails, unused historic electric lighting and rough floors, and the dancing shadows from my lantern playing on the sides. A gent said he saw a figure, and described it to us all.
>
> I suspected, from his description, that he'd seen the spirit of Jeremiah Wilson. Fortunately we were later able to go to our office where I had a photograph of Jeremiah Wilson [for comparison]. The gent said it was a younger version of the man he'd seen in the cave. [interview on Live 90.5 Radio, 2014]

The Jenolan Caves blogsite provides a further ghostly encounter told by yet another Caves Guide, Alan:

> I was taking a group through the Imperial Cave one evening, and we stopped to wait for everyone to catch up. Uneasily, a young couple came up to me and started telling me that they had just been in Caves House dining room for dinner, and something strange had happened.
>
> As the tour group gathered around us, the woman said that when they were sitting at dinner, her partner said to her, 'There's a woman over there, staring at us.' Well, no one else could see the woman. So I asked the man, 'What did she look like?'

Jenolan Caves, N.S.W.

The man replied, 'She looked to be in her 40s or 50s, in period dress of around 100 years ago. Her hair was pulled severely up and back.'

I explained that the apparition roughly fit the description of Lucinda Wilson. She and her husband Jeremiah built the original Caves House, and she was, more or less, the accommodation manager. [www.jenolancaves.org.au/blog/]

The original Caves House where Lucinda worked was located alongside the Jenolan Caves, but was partially destroyed by fire. In 1896, the new rambling, 4-storey, guest-house complex was built from limestone quarried on the site. It is today recognized as one of the finest, large guest-houses still functioning, and received heritage protection in 2004.

It was at the original Caves House that public servant William Ridley recuperated after falling 56ft (17m) through a hole in the Nettle Cave to the floor of the Imperial Cave below in 1887.

Visitors today still hear about Ridley's remarkable survival, and his 'route' to the Imperial Cave is popularly known as Ridley's Shortcut.

However, Ridley's fame may be causing irritation to at least one ethereal occupant of the caves, namely John (Jack) Edwards, who was employed as a guide at Jenolan when this incident occurred.

Jack Edwards became a Jenolan guide in 1886 and spent 22 years working with James Wiburd and Jeremiah Wilson. He lived with his family in a house about three-quarters of a mile (1,200m) away up a steep track in the Jenolan reserve, high above the main road.

Jack worked long hours — 8.30am to 9.00pm — often not returning home until midnight, yet rarely does he rate so much as a mention during cave tours.

Meanwhile, Ridley's fall and stories about Jeremiah Wilson and James Wiburd are told over and over again to new Caves visitors.

Hardly surprising that Jack may feel a bit 'put out'.

Shortly before Christmas in 1908, Jack had stopped to light a cigarette during his long walk along the track towards home. He was later found unconscious, lying on the road immediately below the track.

Perhaps he had dozed off and fell, or maybe he was struck by a falling boulder. No-one knows. He died in the early hours of the following morning.

More than a century after Jack's death, a television cameraman was filming a documentary in the Imperial Cave and was told the story of Ridley's Shortcut. The cameraman also used an EVP (Electronic Voice Phenomena) digital recorder, which 'caught' two messages from a similar voice during filming.

The first message was: 'The crystal grows an inch in a thousand years."

This was a typical tour guide statement and was presumed to be from one of the ghostly guides. But which one?

The next EVP recording, in the same voice, confirmed he was a guide: "My name is John Edwards, not Ridley."

He didn't say so, but no doubt Edwards was thinking: "Twenty two years of hard work and long hours until the day I died, yet Ridley gets all the attention just because he fell over!"

Jeremiah Wilson also had something important to impart to the living, but he chose a most unusual way of doing so.

A Canadian lady was visiting Australia with her daughter and granddaughter. They traveled in a camper-van, taking their time and visiting tourist spots that appealed to them. They called into Jenolan and took one of the cave tours.

> Towards the end of the tour she said, 'I bet there's some really interesting stories about Jenolan,' and the Guide replied 'Oh, yes, we do delve into that on one particular tour, our 'Legends, Mysteries & Ghost' tour.
>
> He mentioned a particular story, known to all the Guides, about a group who had come into a cave and saw a little girl, aged about 8, who was wearing a white dress. She was a ghost because they described her 'dissipating down the stairs.'
>
> Some were really worried that they had to walk past that section, and they said 'No, we don't want to go there, we'll go back the way we came in! And they did!'

The Canadian woman explained to the Guide that she was a 'ghost whisperer'– she worked as someone who clears

Jenolan Caves, N.S.W.

ghosts from people's houses, releasing their spirits so they are free to go to the light. She had recently been working in a chalet in France.

The Canadian ladies departed, but a few weeks later they returned, very excited, to Jenolan Caves.

> They said that they had an interesting passenger, a hitch-hiker, who said his name was Jeremiah Wilson [Jenolan's first tour Guide from 1867 to 1900]. As luck had it, they ran into the same Guide that took them on the 'Imperial' tour, and she told him the story of Jeremiah.
>
> She reported 'He said some things that don't really make much sense to me and perhaps you could shed some light on it. He said that he didn't lose his mind and that it was a plot to get rid of him so Fred could have his job. He also said that he didn't steal any horses.'

What the Canadian lady reported referred to little-known facts about the final year (1900) of Jeremiah's career. Even most of the current tour guides knew nothing about them!

In 1900, it was claimed Jeremiah had gone crazy after becoming lost in the Jubilee cave he was exploring. His brother Fred rescued him and did, indeed, become his successor.

And yes, Jeremiah had been accused of stealing horses!

He appeared before the Bathurst Circuit Court on 11 October, 1900 and pleaded guilty—not to stealing the horses, but to having received them as stolen goods. His defense lawyer claimed 'he had been the dupe of someone else'...and that he had been more sinned against than having sinned.

Even so, he was sentenced to fifteen months hard labor in Bathurst Gaol. While incarcerated, his property at Oberon was sold due to bankruptcy.

With remissions, Jeremiah emerged from the prison a year and a week later. He was a broken shadow of the fine strong man he'd once been. He never regained his former self-esteem, withdrew from company, and was regularly seen sitting with head bowed.

GHOSTS DOWN UNDER

Jeremiah died in 1907. Perhaps he had been waiting all those years for a sympathetic 'ghost-whisperer's ear so he could finally set the record straight.

'He didn't lose his mind, and he didn't steal any horses.'

≈

*The 'Legends, Mysteries & Ghosts' tour
runs every second Saturday night.*

Site details:
http://www.jenolancaves.org.au/the-caves/cave-tour-timetable/regular-tour-timetable/

☼

32. A Ghost May be Heard ...

'stories that would 'make your blood curdle'

The Barcoo River is an inland stream in Western Queensland that flows through the black soil Channel Country to join the Cooper Creek, which, in very wet years, empties into Lake Eyre in South Australia.

Permanent waterholes along the Barcoo ensure adjoining properties have highly productive land for fattening cattle and raising sheep.

One such property, Ruthven Station of about 40,000acres is 30 km southwest of Isisford, includes the Wilga Waterhole within it boundaries. The Wilga Waterhole is known for its reliable water supply when other sources almost run dry.

It is also renowned for something else. It has a century-old reputation for being terrifyingly, spine-chillingly, haunted!

> Drovers and others who camped there reckoned they heard awful shrieks coming from the waterhole at night. ['Tales of the Bush', Narromine News, 18 July 1928, p.4]

Mr T. A. ('Scottie') Gray, who once worked on Ruthven, explains how he came to reside temporarily at the Wilga Waterhole in 1919:

GHOSTS DOWN UNDER

I was about 36 years of age when I went to Ruthven as jackeroo, and was given many jobs by Mr Ramage, the manager, which he would not give to any of the younger fellows.

One day he came to me, and said 'Are you afraid of ghosts? Do you believe in them?' I replied that I was neither frightened of them, nor believed in them. So he told me to pack my kit, take three horses, and get off to the [Wilga] shed as boundary rider.

At that time I was not aware of the fact that no one would have the job on, or live there, and I was blissfully ignorant of its evil reputation. [Scottie Gray in Longreach Leader, 9 December 1941, p.37]

The Wilga hut stood on the banks of the waterhole. It was a two-roomed shanty built of split logs with a large fireplace (which Scottie had to rebuild).

The Wilga Waterhole

He lived there alone for more than six months, but he was never lonely. The Wilga hole was on the track used by drovers, shearers, stockmen, carriers and swagmen [tramps], as they rode or walked between reliable water sources heading south to stock markets, homes and jobs. It was customary to have drovers and stockman refresh their livestock at the Wilga Waterhole and camp overnight on its banks before moving on.

Scottie Gray offers his further reflections on his time there:

Of course, I had to put up with the weird stories told to me by passing travellers, all of which varied considerably. Some swaggies [swagmen], to whom I offered a bed for the night, reckoned they would not dare sleep along that side of the creek after sundown, which was far from being encouraging to me. But I hung on, although some of the stories would make your blood curdle. [Scottie Gray in Longreach Leader, 9 December 1941, p.37]

After spending ten years in Australia, Scottie Gray returned to live in his native Scotland in 1929. His recollections of his time working at the Wilga Waterhole on Ruthven was prompted by an article he read called 'Ghosts I Have Seen' which had been published in the Longreach Leader in December, 1940 and sent to him by a friend. At the time of writing his recollections he was 59 years old.

Whilst there were, and remain today, many variations of the Wilga ghost story, it has one remarkably consistent attribute – the tormented presence is heard but not seen.

In 1928, 'Red Ned' wrote of the Wilga ghost's history in the Narromine News:

Eighty years back, the blacks [indigenous Aboriginals] would not come within yards of it and reckoned that a big debbil-debbil [devil] lived there. People who once heard the awful shrieks never camped there a second time, as the weird noise was too much for their nerves. ['Tales of the Bush', Narromine News, 18 July 1928, p.4]

'Red Ned's reference to 'eighty years back' suggests the Wilga ghost was around in 1848. He also made another observation:

'The blacks had heard the noises long before white man came on the scene.'

'Red Ned' also mentioned Milbung Tommy, an aboriginal who is buried on the banks of the Wilga Waterhole, whose grave he had personally seen.

Australian author E. J. Banfield — writing in 1941 as 'Beachcomber' — suggested that even trying to trace the earliest account of the Wilga phenomena was impossible because it occurred so long ago.

...the first white man who heard them cannot even be

remembered. ['Wailing at the Waterhole,' Sunday Mail (Brisbane), 9 March 1941, p.5]

In 1941, 'Beachcomber' provided a then-50-year-old account of two shearers making their way to the Wellshot sheds, north of Longreach, who camped overnight by the Wilga Waterhole:

> Their horses hobbled and grazing at leisure, the two men made tea over their campfire, ate their damper and salt beef ... they smoked and talked while the hours crept on ...
>
> The fire bedded down to coals and lost much of its cheery glow ...silence fell upon the two men and, wakeful, they continued to sit. About them the bush was stilled ... the gentle breeze died and the branches of the coolibahs [trees] about the waterhole ceased to rustle.
>
> Silence everywhere and then soft, distant wailing ... it grew nearer, louder. Straining ears of the astonished men could not detect how many cries in different keys there seemed to be. Fiends from hell might have made such cries and shrieks, but humans never!
>
> Rolling ever nearer, at last the shrieks and screams seemed to come from out of the waterhole beside which they were camped and then to arise from the very ground beneath their feet.
>
> When it seemed that the two thoroughly frightened shearers, who stood rooted in their tracks, could no longer listen without losing their reason, the shrieking fell in volume until again it was merely a weird wailing.
>
> As it diminished the noise left the spot on which they had camped and retreated in the direction of the waterhole itself. It ceased, completely, utterly, and about them once more was the silence of the bush. Not a ripple marked the surface of the lagoon whence the noise retreated. [Beachcomber, 'Wailing at the Waterhole', Sunday Mail magazine, 9 March 1941, p.5]

'Scottie' Gray, who lived in the Wilga hut, also repeated a first-hand account told to him by a carrier hauling a load of wool bales with a team of horses:

> Carriers who have been compelled to halt in the [Wilga] paddock overnight sleep, for safety, on top of the bales of wool, and I have heard from a carrier's own lips that on one occasion he was

Central West, Queensland

awakened in the middle of the night by a terrific noise as of thunder, and the wailing of something passing backward and forward overhead.

He and his mates could see nothing, yet the noise and wailing continued. Becoming frightened, they got down, left everything, even their rifles, and bolted for the shed.

In the morning they went to yoke up, but found that their 30-odd horses were gone, and these were found later in another paddock, four miles away. [Scottie Gray in Longreach Leader, 9 December 1941, p.37]

Another first-hand account comes from 'Belah,'- a correspondent to the Narromine News in October, 1934.

'Now, I do not believe in ghosts, but I have heard the screams which have been so much discussed wherever Western [Queensland] men congregate, and I know for a fact that stock will not camp on the banks of the Wilga waterhole.' ['Belah' in 'Tales of the Bush', Narromine News, 26 October 1934, p. 6]

Many accounts tell how some livestock become unsettled at night if held near the Wilga Waterhole, not just on evenings when the 'noises' were present. 'Scottie' Gray writes: 'while sheep quietly graze, cattle and horses always break a fence, and get out.'

'Belah,' also recalled another occasion when he tried to calm a mob of old milking cows close to the waterhole. He thought nothing would frighten them ...

'Everything went well,' he wrote, 'until about 9 p.m. when they started to rush and ring. In the morning we were a good three mile from camp, and when the horse tailers returned they informed me the horses had also made a break during the night and were found, badly rung with the hobbles, standing shivering in a corner about five miles from the camp.' ['Belah' in 'Tales of the Bush', Narromine News, 26 October 1934, p.6]

'Red Ned' also related that 'camping herds of cattle [at Wilga Waterhole] even when rounded-up somewhere out on the Downs, would keep the tailers going all night as they refused to lie down.'

If ghosts are departed spirits, reluctant to leave the site of their earthly demise, does the Wilga Waterhole have any tragic incidents that keep those tortured souls shrieking?

Of course! 'Belah' believes he knows who the ghost is. First, though, he established his credentials ...

> I was born in Barcaldine, and my father had been in the sheep-breeding business in the Central-west [of Queensland] for the past 40 years. I have been in touch with the old hands all my life, so I am in a position to give you all the facts believed to be true concerning the Wilga waterhole.
>
> About 70 years back a man named Wilfred was shepherding sheep for the late Jimmy Tyson and lived in a hut on the south side of the [Wilga] waterhole ...while Wilfred was living there a mob of wandering blacks [indigenous Aboriginals] camped alongside the yards where the sheep were kept and during the night they began molesting* the animals. (* in those days, the word 'molesting' meant 'to pester or harass')
>
> Wilfred went across and tried to make them shift camp. A row started, one word brought on another and Wilfred was murdered. Then his body was thrown into the Wilga waterhole where it was found three days later by some drovers... They took the body from the water and buried it at a spot between the hut and the waterhole. When these drovers reached Mount Marlow they reported the murder...
>
> Before the murder of the shepherd, the Wilga lagoons were one of the main meeting places in those parts for the aborigines, as fish and wildfowl were plentiful. ['Belah' in 'Tales of the Bush', Narromine News, 26 October 1934, p. 6]

But there are other possibilities.

A correspondent with Brisbane's Sunday Mail, Mr T Gill, wrote that he had spoken to a jackeroo who claimed to have 'heard the Wilga screams.'

> 'No one could explain the screams,' he added, 'but one story frequently told was that of a young boy employed by a teamster many years ago who was sent to bring in the horses.
>
> He did not return, and although searched for, was never found. Some considerable time afterwards his body, mangled by wild pigs, was found at the waterhole. It is said that 'the screams now heard are his screams for help.'' [Sunday Mail, Brisbane, 16 March 1941, p. 5]

Scotsman, T.A. Gray (Scottie), who once resided in the Wilga hut and heard stories that would 'make your blood curdle' recalls hearing of another death which took place in the hut he occupied:

> 'It is said a boundary rider there went mad and after killing his wife and daughter, hid them down a well, and that it is his mad cries that are heard.' [Longreach Leader, 9 December 1942, p.37]

Next, a suicide. One of the most popular stories, according to 'Strutt' who commented on the Wilga ghost in Sydney's World's News...

> 'is that of a swagman who went insane after drinking some of the local 'jungle juice' [home-made brew] and cut his throat beneath a tree on the bank of the Wilga hole.' [World's News, 4 August 1945, p.19]

Two further deaths are nominated on an internet website:

> 'a few early settlers speculated that it was the ghost of the explorer Ludwig Leichhardt, who passed away on his final, fatal expedition.'

> 'A later theory suggested the ghost of a youth named Toby Coleman who became lost in the bush many kilometers from the waterhole. All that was ever found of him was one leg. The theory contends that his ghost haunts the waterhole looking for that missing limb.' [www.chapelhill.homeip.net/Family History/Others]

Finally, in our gruesome death count, there's Milbung Tommy, an aboriginal who was buried in a grave near the Wilga Waterhole according to 'a couple of fellows who worked at Ruthven,' and seen by 'Red Ned.'

That's a total of seven reported deaths spread over 170 years – not a single one of them witnessed by any of our published correspondents, but all now part of the Wilga Waterhole folklore. Some may be duplicates of others, or simply grafted on to the core account in the retelling of the Wilga story which has since grown, flourished and fruited.

But there is no doubt about the existence of the wailing phenomena.

'Many years ago,' wrote 'Beachcomber' in 1941, 'the story arose that they were made by a bunyip.' (The bunyip is a large mythical creature from Australian Aboriginal mythology, said to lurk in swamps, billabongs, creeks, riverbeds, and waterholes.)

'Beachcomber' immediately dismissed the bunyip theory:

> No such comfortable explanation of the happenings in the Wilga Waterhole is acceptable. Noises made by any creature likely to have been seen by persons in the past days of Australia do not, as far as records go, remotely resemble the yelling and screaming that arises to curdle the blood of the unwary who have camped beside this waterhole on the Barcoo.' ['Beachcomber,' Sunday Mail magazine, 9 March 1941, p.5]

Another reason to exclude the 'bunyip theory' is that none of the many who have heard the 'yelling and screaming' phenomena claim to have seen either person or creature in or about the waterhole.

'Not even a flock of demented kookaburras ['Laughing Jackasses,' which terrified the first Europeans] could make such noises,' wrote 'Beachcomber,' 'or any other Queensland birds!' slamming the door shut on two potential explanations.

Similarly, he rejects the 'subterranean channel' theory, wherein the Wilga waterhole is connected underground 'in some fashion' to another, and the water rushing through this channel 'under certain conditions' account for the shrieking and yelling noises which have frightened so many.

> 'This theory has failed to establish any ground for acceptance,' 'Beachcomber' wrote.

Another Australian bird has been named as the source of the screaming phenomena – the Powerful Owl, 'our most raucous-voiced bush bird', the largest of all Australian owls:

> The mysterious blood-curdling screams were discovered to be the work of the Powerful Owl ... Its screams in the stillness of the bush at night have to be experienced to be appreciated. [Andrew Nicholson, weirdaustralia.com/2014/03/30, 30 March 2014]

However the habitat of the Powerful Owl—according to ornithologists—is in the forests east of the Great Dividing

Range to the coast from Queensland to South Australia – not on the inland Central Western plains of Queensland.

Another explanation plucked bare!

So the Wilga Waterhole hauntings remain unique – heard but not seen over a period of many years, and with no viable earthly explanation.

'Old bushmen who knew the water hole were content to avoid it,' Beachcomber wrote in 1941.

If you ignore his counsel, remember ...

their ghosts may be heard as you pass ...

Indeed! Hopefully this book of Australian ghost stories demonstrates that, wherever you may roam, ghosts may be heard (and seen) all over this vast brown land!

B.W.

References Consulted

Books

Brennan, Martin: Reminiscences of the Goldfields and Elsewhere, (Sydney, 1907)

Brookes, Dame Mabel: Crowded Galleries, (London, 1956)

Buchanan, Stuart: The Lighthouse Keepers, (Sanford, Qld., 1994)

Clemens, Vera P: Interesting Facts of the Hanging Rock, (Kyneton, 1970s)

Cusack, Frank: Australian Ghost Stories, (Melbourne, 1967)

Davis, Richard: Great Australian Ghost Stories, (Sydney, 2000)

Emberg, Joan & Buck Ghostly Tales of Tasmania, (Launceston, 1991)

Hack, Helen: The Mystery of the Mayanup Poltergeist, (Hesperian, 2000)

Hill, Dawn: Edge of Reality, (Pan Books, 1987)

Hooper, F C.: Australian Dictionary of Biography, Vol. 1, (M.U.P, 1966)

Howard-Wright, Miriam: Eyewitness, Australian Ghosts, (Artlook Publishers, 1980)

Johnson. David: Lost Prospect, (Adelaide, 2014)

Liston, Carol: Campbelltown: The Bicentennial History, (Sydney, 1988)

Lovell, Patricia: No Picnic, An Autobiography, (Macmillan, 1995)

McConville, Chris: Hanging Rock – a History, (Melbourne, 2017)

McCulloch, Janelle Beyond the Rock, The Life of Joan Lindsay, (Echo Publishing, 2017)

Miller, Julie & Osborn, Grant: Something Is Out There, (Sydney, 2010)

Montgomery, J. G.: Haunted Australia: Ghosts of the Great South Land, (Pennsylvania, 2016)

Parsons, Vivienne: Australia Dictionary of Biography, Vol. 2, (Melbourne, 1976)

Pinkney, John: Haunted, The Book of Australian Ghosts, (Melbourne, 2005)

Poynter, J.R.: Australian Dictionary of Biography, Vol.13, M.U. P., 1993

Kirkwood, Ray: Variant Breed: Confessions of a Light-Keeper, (Wordclay, 2010)

Rogers, N: A New Year Cruise on the Queensland Coast, (c. 1888)

Scott, Thomas: Travels among Gold and Cannibals in Western Australia, (Perth, W.A.)

St. John, Jeff: The Inside Outsider: The Jeff St.John Story, (Starman Books, 2015)

Steward, Alexander: Reminiscences of Illawarra, (Wollongong, 1984)

Stewart, Nellie: My Life's Story, (Sydney, 1923)

Sullivan, Darnley: Ghosts of Australia, (ebook, 2016)

Talbot, Don: Ghostly Tales of Toowoomba, (Toowoomba, 2004)

Tim the Yowie Man: Haunted and Mysterious Australia, (Sydney, 2017)

Toner, Alan: Paranormal Australia, (ebook, 2014)

Vincent, Liz: Ghosts of Picton Past, (Picton, 2004)

Welch, J H (Major): Quarantine Station, Point Nepean,(Sorrento, 1968)

Wilson, Robert: Canberra Cavalcade, (Canberra, 1996)

Wilson, Robert: A-Z of Australian Towns & Cities, (Weldon, 1989)

Illustrated Guide to Australian Places, (Sydney, 1995)

Magazines & Newspapers

Adelaide Mail, 28 December 1929

Advertiser, The (Adelaide) 17 October 1929

Advocate, The, 22 August 1885

Age, The (Melbourne), 16 April 1981

Argus, The, (Melbourne), 5 March 1888, 15 January 1902 & 15 January 1954

Artlook Magazine, April, 1980

Australasia Post, 1 March 1956

Australian, The, 23 September 1826

Bathurst Free Press, 26 December 1857

Blackwood Times, The 3rd June 1955

Braidwood Review, The 12 April 1921

Campbelltown-Macarthur Advertiser, 21 June, 2006

Canberra Times, 25 February 1984

Cessnock Eagle and South Maitland Recorder, 6 May 1921

Clipper, The, 19 & 26 August 1893

Courier Mail (Brisbane), 24 December 1946

Evening News (Sydney), 14 April 1921

Evening Penny Post (Goulburn), 21 April 1921

Geelong Advertiser, 25 June 1874

Glen Innes Examiner, 14 April 1921

Herald Sun Weekend Magazine (Melb.) 28 April 2018

Illawarra Mercury, 17 September 1920

Junee Southern Cross, 20 August, 2014

Lancefield Courier 31 October 1872

Leader, The (Melbourne), 10 March 1888

Longreach Leader, 9 December 1941

Maitland Daily Mercury, 11 May 1921

Mount Alexander Mail, 16 November 1874

Narromine News, 18 July 1928

Newcastle Morning Herald 11 August 1917 & 20 April 1921

Northern Star (Lismore, NSW), 3 May 1921

People Magazine 12 October 1960

Queanbeyan Age, 20 July 1876 & 19 July 1910

Smith's Weekly, 23 September 1933

Sunday Herald Sun,(Melb.) 29 April 2018

Sunday Mail (Brisbane), 9 February 1941

Sunday Mail, Brisbane (magazine), 9 March 1941

Sunday Times, (Sydney) 15 May 1921

Sydney Gazette 6 April 1811

Sydney Mail, 31 July 1935

Sydney Morning Herald, 22 & 26 April 1921

The World's News, (Sydney), 27 July 1937

Truth (Melbourne), 22 January 1972

Wagga Daily Advertiser 7 July 2014

Who Weekly, 10 June 1996

Windsor and Richmond Gazette, 27 January 1928

Yass Courier, 19 July 1876,

Online

abovetopsecret.com

Forte magazine (online) July 2016

http://realparanormalexperiences.com

http://www.starweekly.com.au ((Paul Levey)

https://portarthur.org.au

https://weirdaustralia.com/2014/03/30 (Andrew Nicholson . 30 March 2014)

Lighthouses of Australia Monthly Bulletin, (April 2001)

Moustache Magazine (online), (Dominic Cansdale, 23 October 2014)

ttps://www.clarkefieldcoachandhorsesinn.com

www.aussietowns.com.au

www.chapelhill.homeip.net/Family History/Others

www.jenolancaves.org.au/blog/ (Ashley Hall)

www.theparanormalguide.com/blog/entally-estate

Other

'Haunted' TV documentary series (Dr Maurice Marsh, 1989)

'Rewind' (Justin Murphy, compere) ABC TV, (August 2004)

Ghosts of Port Arthur, Peter Richman Productions, (video documentary, 2003)

'Haunting Australia' Bill Tabone, TV series, 2015

Live 90.5 Radio (interview, 2016)

Parasearch UK Radio (Penny Morgan, 1 November 2017)

Rebecca Betts, Rye, Victoria

Also by Barry Watts

Get it at Amazon
as ebook or paperback

www.ingramcontent.com/pod-product-compliance
Lightning Source LLC
Chambersburg PA
CBHW020421010526
44118CB00010B/351